SOLDIER, SAILOR, LIVE OR DIE

SOLDIER, SAILOR, LIVE OR DIE

Noel Davidson

AMBASSADOR

BELFAST, NORTHERN IRELAND
GREENVILLE, USA

Soldier, Sailor, Live or Die
© Copyright 2001 Noel Davidson

ISBN 1   84030 105 8

Ambassador Publications
a division of
Ambassador Productions Ltd.
Providence House
Ardenlee Street,
Belfast,
BT6 8QJ
Northern Ireland
www.ambassador-productions.com

Emerald House
427 Wade Hampton Blvd.
Greenville
SC 29609, USA
www.emeraldhouse.com

CONTENTS

FOREWORD

The life story of any Christian should always dwell on what God has done. It's not a presenation of our activities, but will rather significantly magnify the work of God. Obviously, the human element is in the story, but the major part has to be what has been accomplished by the grace of God. This book does exactly that.

'Soldier, Sailor, Live or Die' is a journey in the life of Jackie Dickey. Travelling on that journey, through the pages and chapters, one can trace the hand of God upon his life, especially in those situations when Jackie was oblivious of His presence, yet there was continually the unseen hand of God, providing protection from accidents at sea as well as bombs on the streets of Belfast.

His early life, just after the war, was reminiscent of many at that time. The closeness of family, the love of a grandmother and the influence of the Boys Brigade, all helped in the development of a young life. Joining the Navy at sixteen proved to be a determining factor, even then Jackie showed a determination to see his dreams fulfilled that same determination was evident years later when he sought to find a wife.

Sadly, in this new environment he would learn to drink more than coke. He not only saw the world but also enjoyed its pleasure. Pleasures so called which would eventually mean coutning the cost of attempting suicide while serving with the Ulster Defence Regiment. Jackie was 'the drunken sailor'. However, that would all change.

Recvovering from excessive drinking while on holiday he began to read a Gideon New Testament, which somehow had found its way into the suitcase loaned to Jackie by his uncle. What he read, resulted in him calling on the Lord to save him, his salvation experience was so comprehensive that the taste for the devil's liquor left him immediately.

Obviously, the change in his life was soon apparent to all his friends, with the love for alcohol being replaced by a love for people, especially those, in the forces, who he visited in their barracks as well as hospitals where he befriended them with feeling and sincerity. Sailor, as he was affectionately known, used the visits to tell of God's love.

Jackie having married Mandy would find that Christianity did not mean immunity from the problems of life, together they experienced Christianity wearing working clothes, but through the joys and sorrows their story is about the grace and provision of Almighty God. This book is both refreshing and challenging. It is a testimony to the fact that those who trust in Jesus, irrespective of background or circumstances can become new creations in Christ Jesus.

What you are going to read demonstrates that nothing is too hard for God.

Eric McComb
Superintendent of Elim Churches in Ireland

INTRODUCTION

'God must surely love the ordinary people' I heard someone quip once, 'for He made an awful lot of us.'

We know what he meant, but on the other hand, is there any such thing as an 'ordinary' person? For just below the surface of many of the seemingly unremarkable people we meet there lies a fascinating and remarkable story.

And such a person is Jackie 'Sailor' Dickey. He has had a wealth of experience in his life to date, having survived a series of life threatening situations, but if you met him on the footpath, you wouldn't immediately turn your head to look after him, exclaiming as you did so, "Hey, isn't he some guy?"

Or if you were standing at the kerb, waiting to cross the street and he drove past in his car, you wouldn't feel any need to follow it with your eyes until it disappeared around a bend or behind a bus, thinking all the while, "My isn't that a marvellous motor!"

No. Jackie just looks like an ordinary fellow. And there would appear to be hundreds of them about. Your Mr. A.V.Erage.

Yet when asked if he knew Jackie Dickey and Mandy, his wife, a local pastor replied, "Know them! Of course I know them! They should be in Hebrews Eleven that pair!"

So why, then, should such an apparently ordinary man, living in an apparently ordinary house, and driving an apparently ordinary car, be nominated for The Bible's roll of honour?

The answer lies in the fact that this 'apparently ordinary' man has had an absolutely extraordinary experience with an Almighty God.

It has all to do with the fact that it is said of Jesus in the scriptures that 'the common people heard him gladly.'

Jackie has been with Jesus. And heard him gladly.

And that is what makes the difference.

When I first met Jackie and Mandy and heard their story, I was impressed. Here were two people who had been led to know Christ as Saviour at different times, in different places and in virtually unbelievable ways. And they had also been kept, by the mighty hand of God, through the many ups and downs of life.

So I felt compelled to write this book as a testimony to the saving grace, and sustaining presence, of God.

No life story, though, is only one story. For in addition to the main theme, which is the miracle of salvation and the strength of Christian faith, there are other, at first unrecognised, aspects to this book as well.

Although not setting out to be so, it is a history book. Do you remember the big zinc bath by the big roaring fire in the two-up and two-down terrace houses in the arrow-straight city streets? Or the shipyard and the workingmen's clubs? Or the tragedies of the Troubles?

Although not saying so in the sub-title, this is also an adventure story. For Jackie left home at sixteen, to join the Navy and see the world…

It is also a love story, and the tale of triumph in testing situations.

And yet, but for the preserving grace of God it would never have been written.

For Jackie was thrown from his bicycle in a bomb blast, shot at by snipers, and later became a virtually incurable alcoholic. And in the depths of despair he attempted to take his own life. Not once, but twice…

Jackie and Mandy have been through so much.

It has been a pleasure to work with them and share in their simple faith in their wonderful Saviour.

At our first meeting they assured me that their only aim in having their story recorded was that it should bring glory to God and others to Him.

We all pray that it will.

Noel I. Davidson
June 2001

Chapter One

A HERO COME HOME

"Do we really *have* to be bathed tonight?" young Jackie Dickey asked incredulously, as he watched his mother fill up the big zinc bath, carry it in to the front of the fire, and then top it up with successive kettles of boiling water. "Sure we never get baths in the middle of the week! This is only Thursday night! Saturday night is our bath night!"

Isobel, his mother, looked across at him with a quaint smile. "Yes, that's right, son," she was forced to agree. "But you know that we have all to be well cleaned up for tomorrow, for tomorrow will be special!"

That ended nine-year old Jackie's protest.

His young sister Florence was first into the bath, for girls were always bathed first, and when they were 'decent', the boys followed. Tom, 'the baby', at three years old was next, and when it came Jackie's turn he had to make the best of the cooling bathwater. When mother had finished lathering her three youngest children, one by one, with a slippery bar of Lifebuoy soap, dad dried them one by one with a big towel, which he had warmed at the fire.

Theirs was a happy home in Frome Street, off Dee Street, in East Belfast. Alex and Isobel Dickey had seven of a family, four boys and three girls. Jim, Alex (junior), Marie and Sally were all older than Jackie, Florence and Tom, so they were considered old enough to look after themselves in all matters pertaining to personal hygiene. But 'the three young ones', as their parents called them, all had to be bathed.

And it was Jackie's older brother Alex. who was going to make tomorrow so special. For Alex had just returned from active service in the Far East with the Royal Ulster Rifles, and tomorrow, Friday 7th May, 1965, he was going to be parading, with his regiment, through the centre of the city to a reception in the City Hall.

Jackie hardly slept that night at all. Neither indeed did anybody else in the house.

They had so much to think about, and a lot to anticipate. And there was so much about which they could only speculate.

What would Alex be like now? They wondered. It was almost two years since he had gone away. Would he have changed much? Would he be all sunburnt having been in Borneo, wherever that was? Somebody had told them it was near Hong Kong, but they weren't sure if that was right, and anyway it didn't make much difference for they hadn't a clue where it was either!

Everyone was up early that Friday morning and they were all dressed up in their Sunday best long before it was time to leave, prompting repeated cautions from mother, "Now make sure you don't get your good clothes all messed up before we are ready to go!"

Shortly before half-past ten a group of seven people left Frome Street to walk the mile or more into the city centre.

The three children were openly and unmistakably excited.

The four accompanying adults were more modestly, but still unmistakably, excited.

Florence and Jackie skipped on ahead of the rest with seemingly endless energy and enthusiasm. Walking into central Belfast in the middle of a Friday morning was a welcome change from playing 'chasing' around the playground of Mersey Street Primary School at break-time.

Their parents held Tom between them by the hand, swinging him off his feet every now and again, much to his amusement. They were accompanied, as they were often, by Granny and Granda Gibb, Isobel's parents, who also lived in east Belfast. Granny Gibb wheeled the empty tan-sad, a sixties buggy, for Tom to ride in 'when his wee legs got tired'. There was a regular bus service from where they lived right in to where they were going but the Dickeys didn't have a lot of surplus funds for fares, and apart from that, Granda, who worked in the nearby Harland & Wolff shipyard, and walked to his work every day, insisted that 'the exercise is good for you'

It was important to be in early to find 'a good stand' from where everybody could see everything that happened. This was a red-letter day for the Dickeys, and they were determined to make the most of it.

Granny took control of selecting, and then procuring, a suitable viewing position. When she had decided that six feet of footpath outside the Belfast Telegraph office in Royal Avenue would suit their purposes admirably, she set about staking their claim. Shunting the tan-sad through the already gathering crowds until it was right out at the edge of the pavement, she positioned Jackie and Florence one on either side of it, sitting on the kerb. On surveying the family standing around her she realized that her husband still couldn't see anything from where he was, for Granda Gibb was certainly not Goliath of Gath, so she asked the man beside her, politely, "You wouldn't mind moving over there just a little bit to let my husband in?"

He did, and now all seven could see everything!

Although they had almost an hour to wait before the parade was due to come along the time passed quickly for there was so much, and so many other expectant people, to see, and to comment on. And as they became increasingly aware of the crowds building up behind them, Granda, who had a habit of being at nearly everything long before it was due to begin, kept saying, over and over again, to anyone who would listen, "Isn't it a good job we set out in good time?"

At last the patience of the chattering crowd was amply rewarded. Hundreds of animated conversations were suddenly hushed into silence by the distinctive sound of the marching music of a military band.

"They're coming!" Florence whispered.

"They're coming!" Jackie echoed.

And round the corner, from the York Street end of Royal Avenue, they came.

The first thing Jackie saw was the dog, being led in front of the band by a soldier in uniform. And what immediately struck him was the sheer *size* of the dog! It was huge. In fact it looked nearly as big as some of the calves he had seen on the Pyper's farm that he used to visit, near Ballyhalbert, on the Ards Peninsula, during the summer holidays. He was later to learn that this colossal canine was called Finn Mc Cool and it was the regimental mascot.

Then came the band, in their colourful uniforms, with their shining instruments, playing stirring music.

Jackie and Florence both jumped to their feet, and scanned beyond the band.

Where was their Alex?

Not surprisingly, it was his mother who spotted him first.

"There he is!" she shouted, joyfully. And then all seven seemed to see him at once.

Although still only nineteen, Alex looked such a man in his uniform, marching along, with his back straight, and his head held high. He saw them, but could only give the faintest of smiles of recognition. He was a disciplined soldier, in uniform, on parade. For the two days the regiment had been confined to barracks since returning from their tour of duty, he had been wondering if the family would turn up to see him march through the city. Now he had his question answered, and he felt so proud of them all.

Alex's pleasure at seeing his family encamped on the pavement, however, was minimal compared to the pride and pleasure it gave them to see him. Every eye remained fixed on his marching figure until he disappeared into the distance up Donegall Place, towards the City Hall, where the Lord Mayor had arranged a lunchtime reception for the regiment.

Jackie felt so proud that he cried. Tears of pleasure tumbled down his cheeks.

His big brother was his big hero.

When the noise of the band had faded away, and the crowds had begun to surge out into the street in pursuit of the parade, Jackie looked over at Florence. She was wiping her eyes with the hankie she kept tucked into the sleeve of her Sunday dress. Then when he looked round at the adults he realized that they had all been shedding a tear or two as well. Indeed his dad was still attempting to wipe his face with the back of his hand.

So he hadn't been the only one affected!

All that remained for them to do now was trudge back home, and await the returning soldier son and brother's arrival. His parents had been told in the letter that they had received that Alex would have a period of leave, and how they were looking forward to that!

When they arrived back in Frome Street not one of the seven who had seen their homecoming hero parade so proudly through the city centre had been able to settle to anything. Not one of them was sure whether he or she wanted to sit inside in the parlour or outside on the windowsill. A certain restless anticipation had gripped them all, again.

For they were all waiting for Alex, again.

And eventually all their waiting was rewarded, for eventually he came.

It was late in the afternoon when the man of the moment turned the corner into his home street.

What a thrill!

What rejoicing!

Starting with his mother, Alex junior hugged them all, one by one. There were many tears of joy, many exclamations like, "Great to see you home, son!" or, "You look brilliant in that uniform!" or, "We were all so proud of you today!" And when the news spread like wildfire down the street all the neighbours swarmed up around the door of number twenty, like bees buzzing to enter a hive, all jostling for prime position. Everyone wanted to be first to catch a glimpse of 'young Alex', who had been 'away in the Army.'

It was not only the fact that Alex had returned home safely from active service that made the family so happy, it was what he brought home with him that made some of the younger family members the envy of the neighbourhood.

For the two older sisters, both now teenagers, Alex had bought colourful Chinese dresses.

Marie's dress was blue.

And Sally's dress was red.

How those girls strutted up and down the street in their new frocks, convinced that there was not another girl in the entire city of Belfast as well off, or as well dressed, as either of them!

And how, too, all their friends just gaped in admiration! They had never, they said, seen anything 'just quite so nice', before.

Dresses were just for girls, though.

For the boys of the Dee Street district, it was Jackie's tank that was the centre of attraction.

The returning serviceman had brought his nine-year-old brother a model tank, but this prized present was definitely no ordinary model tank.

Jackie's was a remote-control tank! When you pressed a button it could move backwards and forwards. And even better still, when you pressed another button it actually fired specially prepared plastic bullets!

From being just one of dozens of typical inner city houses, in one of dozens of typical inner city streets, twenty Frome Street suddenly became a meeting place for model lovers within hours! And Jackie fairly glowed with pride, for now the tables had been turned.

For years he used to have to run round to a friend's house in Newcastle Street where he would ask, sheepishly, "Hi, can I play with your Scalectrix racing car set?" or to another friend in Frazer Street where he would enquire, "Can I see your Hornby train set?"

Now these boys, and dozens more, were coming knocking on his door and asking, "Hi, Jackie, can I have a go with your tank?"

Jackie's boyhood hero, back from foreign fields, had made him a boyhood hero, back in his own street!

Chapter Two

GRANNY GIBB

When Jackie was twelve years of age a number of changes took place in his life.

He was well through his first year in Ashfield Boy's Secondary School when his Granda, Tommy Gibb, died.

Then, within months of the sad experience of his Granda's death, came the good news that the Dickey family had been offered a three-bedroomed house in a new housing development at Tullycarnet on the outskirts of the city.

Everyone seemed delighted at the prospect. The thought of three bedrooms and a bathroom, all upstairs, was marvellous! What a change it would be from the two-up and two-down of Frome Street. And there would be no dashing across the yard in the middle of the night to the outside loo either! Fantastic!

The only person who had her reservations about the big flit to Tullycarnet was Mary Gibb. Her husband was gone, and now, all the family whom she had taken to school every day, and cared for until their parents came home from work, were soon going to be gone too. She tried to console herself that 'Yes, it will be great for them', but inwardly she knew that her life, which had once been so full, was suddenly going to end up very empty.

After some family heart-searching it was Jackie who helped resolve the situation. He volunteered to stay behind, to forego the call of Tullycarnet, and live with Granny Gibb.

There were a few days after the big move that Jackie felt a bit cheated, but after he had become accustomed to his new set of circumstances, he loved life with Granny. His early teenage years with her turned out to be some of the happiest, and also the most formative, days of his life.

Jackie thought Granny was great. There was something reassuring and settling about being in her presence, always. She had very long hair but only occasionally did Jackie see it hang down her back. She usually wore it, piled up on the top of her head in what she described as a 'bun'. There was something comforting, too, about the sameness of her dress. Every day she turned out in a long black frock covered by a white apron, which had been starched until it was almost stiff.

Her face, and hands, and house, were always shining.

Although he was so content living there Jackie realized that Granny was finding it tight to keep him, and run the house on her widow's pension, so he began to make enquiries about finding himself a part-time job. After he had asked a few people his friend Roy came round to his house one evening and said that they needed another helper on the lemonade van. Would Jackie be interested in joining him in that? he wondered.

Of course Jackie would be interested! It was just what he had been looking for.

There then followed a period when Jackie worked three days a week after school, and all day Saturday, selling lemonade all over Belfast. His weekly wage for this work was ten shillings, and it always gave him a strange sense of manly pride to present Granny with his hard-earned ten-shilling note when he arrived home on a Saturday night. And when he had handed over his pay, then he waited. If there hadn't been too many bills to settle during the week, Granny handed him a half-crown back. If there had, she kept it all, and Jackie didn't mind in the least. That was why he was working.

From his very earliest days staying with her, Jackie looked forward to Granny's stories in the evening. Mary couldn't read or write, but she could tell stories. No matter whether it had been a free day after school, or a lemonade lorry day, Jackie liked to get home. It was such a cosy consolation, just before bedtime, to sit across the tiny living-room from the ageing woman and listen to her recount what he called 'the stories of the War', with the firelight flickering on her face.

Some of these were sad stories, but her grandson loved them. He was constantly asking her to tell him more of what happened in Belfast during World War 2.

One of Jackie's favourites was to hear Granny describe the night during the Blitz when their house was bombed. When she and 'your Granda' arrived back home, as they thought, after a night spent in an air-raid shelter, their house wasn't there! It didn't exist any more! All that remained, where their house had once been, was a heap of smouldering rubble. It had been flattened by a stray German bomb, which had been aimed at the nearby shipyard.

Another aspect of Granny's wartime experience that Jackie never tired hearing about was what happened when the three sailors lodged with them once, when their ship was in dry dock for repairs.

"It was Tommy who brought them home," she would reflect. "Lovely lads they were, too."

She would pause, as though to recall them more clearly, and then proceed to explain, "It was great fun having them. They often used to bring us food home. I never dared ask them where they got it mind you! I think it was off the ships!"

One night Jackie asked her a question to clear up something he had wondered about more than once.

"Did you ever hear from those sailors again, Granny? I mean did they ever write to you or anything like that?" he enquired.

There was a longer than usual pause before Granny answered that one.

"No, son," she replied at length, with a long, sucking sigh. "We never heard from them again. I think they were all killed in the war."

For the next ten minutes the both of them sat staring into the fire, the only sound to crack open the silence being the rhythmic tick-tock, tick-tock of the big wooden clock on the mantelpiece.

During the week Granny Gibb's stories could have been about almost anything, or almost anybody, but Sunday night's stories were always, invariably, Bible stories.

Although then in his early teens, Jackie never ceased to be captivated when Granny told him Bible stories. She told them with such absolute conviction. Whether it was Noah and the ark, Samson and Delilah, Moses and the burning bush, or Daniel and the burning fiery furnace, they all came across with a natural simplicity that rendered them irresistible.

It was when recounting some of the incidents from the life of Jesus, though, that Mary Gibb was at her storytelling best. It made no difference whether the episode she was relating concerned a powerless man by a pool, a curious character up a tree, or a wondering woman at a well, she ever only spoke of Jesus in hushed, reverent tones denoting a most profound respect, a holy awe.

And when it came to the stories of the cross there was usually a tear in her eye.

"What they done to Jesus was awful, son. It was awful," she would exclaim, her doubtful grammar more than compensated for by her undoubted sincerity. Then she would proceed to tell him, with a solemn nod of the head, "It was all for us, too, you know, son. It was all for us!"

It seemed, too, that the Sunday night sessions, which touched upon some aspect of the death of Christ on Calvary, had a profound effect upon Granny Gibb. They seemed to do something to her vocal chords, or oil up her singing voice, for at least for the Monday and Tuesday of that week she could be heard singing, both softly and sweetly. Regardless of whether Jackie was just coming in, just going out, or just planning to spend the evening lounging about, he heard her. And there could be no doubting either what was her favourite piece.

It was,

'On a hill far away, stood an old rugged cross,
The emblem of suffering and shame;
And I love that old cross, where the dearest and best
For a world of lost sinners was slain,'

Jackie often smiled to himself, when he heard her sing, for he was convinced that if there were more than two verses to the hymn, Granny had never heard of the others. At least all she ever sang were two verses and the chorus, repeated over and over again.

The second verse in Mary's repertoire was the final one of the hymn. This verse she would render with a sense of dignity and loyalty. She surely meant it when she sang,

'To the old rugged cross I will ever be true,
Its shame and reproach gladly bear;
Then He'll call me some day to my home far away,
When His glory for ever I'll share.'

Each of these verses would be followed by the chorus, sung with a strange warmth, in a kind of personal dedication, it appeared to her live-in-grandson.

So I'll cherish the old rugged cross
Till my trophies at last I lay down;
I will cling to the old rugged cross
And exchange it some day for a crown'

In addition to his Granny, there were two other people, both men, whose lives were to leave a lasting impression on young Jackie Dickey. And they were both officers in Belfast's 64th Boy's Brigade Company in Westburn Presbyterian Church on the Newtownards Road.

The first of these men was the Captain, Davy Mills. Jackie held this man in high regard. He had fought in the Second World War, and that made him extraordinary immediately. It put him in the same class as big brother Alex, an ex-service superhero.

Perhaps it was a throwback to his army days, but this B.B. Captain was a strict disciplinarian. Rules were rules, and you kept them, or you were out. And one of these rules was that you must attend the Sunday morning Bible Class in Church, and repeat your memory verse off perfectly, before you were permitted to play football on Monday night.

So it often happened that Jackie would end up running around Granny's house on a Sunday morning, looking for his socks, and repeating aloud, "For God so loved the world that he gave his only begotten Son, that whosoever believeth on him should not perish, but have everlasting life."

When he had found the socks and put them on he would then ask, "Well, Granny, what do you think? Will I be playing this week, or not?"

It was important for Jackie to keep his place in the football squad, for it was Roy Stewart who played for Glentoran, who coached the team, and all the boys in East Belfast loved their local team, 'The Glens'.

This player was the second man whom he idolised. And although Jackie was no more than an average player who usually managed to kick the ball in the right direction at the right time, most of the time, if Roy Stewart should comment to the red-faced teenager at the end of match, "You had a good game there tonight, Jackie," the lad basked in the glow of that remark for about three weeks!

And no matter what any day had held, of joy or disappointment, pleasure or pain, Granny always advised Jackie to 'say his prayers' at bedtime. To help him in this endeavour, she had placed strategically above his bed a little cardboard picture, which he had been given years before as a prize, in Dee Street Salvation Army Citadel The picture was of a boy holding what looked to the envious Jackie like a wonderful yacht with big white sails, and the words below it were,

'All this day Thy hand hath led me,
And I thank Thee for Thy care;
Thou hast clothed me, warmed and fed me,
Listen to my evening prayer.'

For the first six months with Granny, Jackie had slipped down on to one knee beside his bed, squinted with one opened eye at this fading picture and raced through the words like a fire-tender on a 999 call.

When he complained to Granny that he thought that prayer was 'only for babies' she said, "O.K. son, we will learn the Lord's Prayer." Although he had been expected to learn the Lord's Prayer at school Jackie had never given such matters his undivided attention. Now though, with Granny to encourage, he learnt it off word perfectly.

As he advanced into teenage Jackie still repeated, every evening, before he climbed into bed, and at only about quarter the speed of 'All this day...' for he had to concentrate more on the words,

'Our Father, which art in heaven, hallowed be thy name. Thy Kingdom come. They will be done on earth, as it is in heaven...'

He had a purpose in learning this prayer, too, for Granny had advised him often, "Son, if you are ever in trouble, you can talk to God. Just say the Lord's Prayer."

So it might just turn out to be a useful thing to know.

Chapter Three

BOMBED OFF THE BIKE

It was possibly from a combination of Granny's stories and the often-recounted adventures of his Uncle Robert who had served in the Royal Navy 'during the War', that Jackie decided on what he thought would be a wonderful way to spend his adult life.

When anybody asked him what he was going to do 'when he grew up', his answer was ever the same.

"I am going to join the Navy and see the world!" he told them.

The problem was, though, that he couldn't apply to join the Navy until he was sixteen years old, but he had no desire to remain at school until that age, for two reasons. The first of these was that he didn't really like school all that much, and the second was a much more practical, down-to-earth, concern. Granny needed him to start earning money as soon as possible to help augment their weekly income.

So Jackie Dickey left Ashfield Boy's Secondary School just after he had turned fifteen, and became a message-boy with the 'Belfast Telegraph', a city evening newspaper. His job was to take parcels to the two railway stations in the city, and to ferry prints across to the offices of the 'News Letter', a morning paper, in Donegall Street, when required. To enable him to make all his deliveries he had been provided with a shiny new messenger bicycle with a basket at the front.

Jackie was so proud of his job, and of his bike.

When he had first started in that position, his immediate boss had told him, "This is your bike, Jackie, and it is up to you to look after it. If it is damaged at all, the cost of any repairs will be deducted from your wages."

The new employee vowed to take first class care of his new bike. He would have to. His wages were to be five pounds for a five-and-a half-day week, but if he arrived home some Saturday with any less than that he could imagine that Granny Gibb would probably have a few questions to ask.

A year on the message bike passed quickly, for Jackie had a single goal in view. He wanted to be sixteen, so that he could apply to join the Navy.

When he reached that magic age, he didn't wait long either.

One day in his lunch hour, Jackie walked across the city centre to the Navy recruiting office, and when a cheery officer in an impressive uniform enquired, "Well, young man, how can we help you?" he restated the ambition he had voiced to so many people, so many times, before.

"I want to join the Navy and see the world!" he blurted out.

The officer smiled.

"I think we can help you then," he replied, reassuringly.

After a short question and answer session followed by an equally short form-filling session, Jackie was free to go.

As the recruiting officer was leaving him to the door his last words were, "Thank you for calling, Jackie. You will be hearing from us in a month or two."

As he walked back to work, Jackie Dickey imagined he had just been appointed as an Admiral of the Fleet. He was so very happy. He was about to fulfil his boyhood ambition, in 'a month or two'.

Within that month or two, however, something happened which could have cost the would-be sailor his life.

Monday, 20ᵗʰ March 1972 began as a normal, routine working day, at the beginning of what Jackie had fully expected to be another normal, routine working week. He hadn't yet heard from the Royal Navy but with that to look forward to he had determined to do his best in his work, until the anticipated letter arrived.

It was just a few minutes before midday, that day, and Jackie was sitting on his bike, one toe on the ground, at the traffic lights waiting to turn right into Donegall Street. He had a pack of prints in the basket for the News Letter office. When the red light turned green he would be across the road and on his way…

Suddenly there was a tremendous, blinding flash, followed by a loud bang, which seemed to rumble and echo on and on forever…

Jackie was thrown from his bicycle and across the road.

He was shocked and stunned, and lay there, frozen by fear, for what felt like ages. When he became aware of the mounting commotion around him, he tried to lift his head up to see what was going on, but couldn't. The attempt to move had shown him one thing. He was in pain from head to toe. Every limb he tried to lift, ached.

With something of an effort, Jackie turned his head to one side, and was horrified at what he saw. Shop windows had come crashing out on to the street. Cars and vans had been reduced to mangled masses of metal. An ominous pall of smoke hung over the scene.

The most shocking thing of all was to see what had happened to the people who had been going about their daily business. Some were holding their hands, or blood-soaked handkerchiefs, over horrendous wounds.

Others weren't moving at all. They remained motionless.

Some of them were already lifeless.

They were dead.

There seemed to be blood, and bodies, everywhere.

What Jackie couldn't understand, though, was why everywhere was so quiet.

Why was nobody yelling, or screaming, or crying?

Why the awful silence?

It was only when an ambulance man ran across to where he lay, and bent down to speak to him, that Jackie realized what had happened.

He couldn't hear a word the man said.

The blast had left him temporarily deaf.

Having had previous experience in such situations the ambulance man knew what to do. He leaned right down and yelled into the traumatized teenager's ear, "Are you all right, son?"

Seeing what was happening all around him, Jackie was thankful to be able to shout back, unnecessarily loudly in reply, "Yes, I'm O.K."

"That's good," came the shouted response. "If you don't mind then we will lift you off the road to clear a way for the ambulances."

With that he and a colleague carried Jackie, who was only badly bruised and shaken having been rocketed ten feet along the road by the force of the blast, to somewhere safer. They then tried to make him comfortable, with a blanket wrapped around him, up against a wall on a splintered-glass-littered pavement.

As his senses, and his hearing, gradually returned, a relatively insignificant issue suddenly became a matter of utmost importance to the conscientious message-boy.

His bike!

Where was his bike?

What would happen if it had been all smashed up?

He would get no pay for weeks!

Jackie shouted at a policeman, hurrying past. "Hi, mister, have you seen my bike?"

The policeman gave him a scowl and hurried on. He was trying to cope with the dead and dying and this daft idiot was worried about his bike!

When he was able to force himself to his feet, with the help of the wall behind, Jackie looked for his bike himself. And he saw it, too. It had obviously been blown from below him, tossed up into the air, and had come to rest in sorry shape, thirty feet from where he had been found in the middle of the road.

On recovering sufficiently Jackie was taken home, and granted a few days off to recover from his ordeal.

It was Friday morning when he returned in trepidation to the Belfast Telegraph office in Royal Avenue.

What was his boss going to say about the bike?

He need not have worried.

The boss was a lot more sympathetic than his young message-boy had ever imagined he could have been, and he told him that since the I.R.A. bomb which had killed seven people and maimed many more on that momentous Monday, had been nothing to do with him, they would provide him with another bike. He told him, too, as dozens of people had already done, that he was 'lucky to be alive'.

Jackie knew that.

On the days he had been at home, being pampered by Granny, he had often wondered what would have happened to him if the lights had been green that morning. If they had been, he would probably have been in Donegall Street when the bomb went off.

Jackie had been in trouble that morning, and he didn't have time to put Granny's counsel to the test. He hadn't even been granted a second to breathe a sentence of the Lord's Prayer.

Yet 'Our Father which art in heaven' had faithfully answered his prayer of the night before.

He had delivered him from evil.

Chapter Four

YOU'L NEVER MAKE IT, PADDY

The Navy Recruiting officer kept his word.

Jackie did 'hear from' them, as he had promised.

In late April the long-awaited letter came inviting him to attend for a medical examination. In eager anticipation Jackie duly presented himself for the 'medical' on the specified date, and when he was passed fit, he was furnished with a travel warrant.

Jackie Dickey was instructed to report to the Military Police unit at the Liverpool boat in Belfast docks on 30th May 1972. He was to show them his travel warrant and they would arrange for him to be allowed on board for the first leg of his trip to Plymouth.

He was going to join the Navy to see the world.

The month of May passed in a flurry of preparation and anticipation. So when the day of his departure arrived, Jackie was ready, or at least Jackie thought he was ready, to set out on his big adventure.

He was going to join the Navy to see the world.

Leaving Belfast was more difficult than he had ever expected it to be, though.

Jackie sat out on deck at the stern of the boat, lonely and scared.

As he stared, in a blank numbness, over the rooftops of the city as they began to glow orange in the setting sun, he thought, 'Granny's house is out there somewhere'.

It had been hard leaving her. She was breaking her heart.

Should he just dash down that gangplank and back to her? His heart was torn in two as he looked down at the old battered suitcase she had given him for going away. It had been unearthed in the attic and diligently dusted. It had been Granda Gibb's 'during the war. And it looked like it. Granny had supervised the packing of it, too. She had put things into it, taken them out again, and then put them back in again, dozens of times.

Perhaps he should just go back home to Granny, and his job in the Belfast Telegraph.

He could forget all about joining the Navy. Or seeing the world.

Soon, though, it was too late for a rethink. Or a retreat.

The ship had cast off, and had begun to sail.

A row of people lined the deck rail waving hands and hankies to a group of family and friends on the quay, far below. They were waving hands and hankies back.

Jackie had nobody to wave to. He had said his 'Goodbyes' to his parents, and his Granny Gibb, back at home, and had made his way down to the docks on his own, in the bus.

He was sixteen years and five months old, and felt very much alone.

As the boat glided out of Belfast Lough the lights along the County Down shore began to twinkle on. Darkness was approaching. The loneliness was becoming overpowering.

When Jackie went inside to redeem his food voucher, 'for a meal on board', another lad joined him in the queue. And he spoke to Jackie.

"Hey, are you going to join the Navy?" he enquired. "I'm sure it was you I saw out in the hut before I came on."

"Yes, I am. Are you?" Jackie responded, hardly able to believe that he was not the only one on that boat on the way to Plymouth.

"Yes, I am as well," the stranger replied, and he appeared to be as glad to see Jackie as Jackie had been to see him.

In the course of conversation the would-be sailor from Belfast discovered that this other would-be sailor was from Ballymena. Apparently his ambition, from his earliest days, had been exactly the same as Jackie's.

He had always wanted to join the Navy and see the world.

Although the crossing became rougher later in the night, although the three hour wait for the train in Liverpool station in the cold grey light of early morning was chilly, and although the nine hour train journey from

Liverpool to Plymouth became very tedious, still Jackie completed the journey with a lighter heart.

His Ballymena friend and he talked the whole way. And after a few passing remarks about left families and left jobs they had only one topic of conversation.

They talked incessantly about joining the Navy. And speculated incessantly about seeing the world.

What would it be like? Where would they be sent?

Africa? America? Australia?

Hong Kong?

Jackie said that he would like to go to Hong Kong, for his big brother had been 'out near there, in the Army.'

The fantasies all finished with a sudden jolt, however, when the train hit the buffers in Plymouth.

A motley stream of new recruits tumbled out of the carriages, and carried a motley assortment of bags and cases out through the draughty door marked EXIT.

Jackie was one of the first to step out. He was so obviously a novice.

When a roll had been called and the welcoming officer was satisfied that all his charges had arrived they were directed to the waiting minibuses.

A policeman, who must have heard Jackie's Northern Ireland accent when responding to the roll stepped up beside the rather flustered sixteen year old and said, "I don't think you will ever make it in the Navy, Paddy, son, but if *you* think you can, get into that bus over there. You see the one I mean. The big blue one with Royal Navy painted all down the side of it!"

Jackie climbed up into the minibus, feeling rather despondent. That was a far from promising start to his Navy career.

His misery only lasted a mile or two, however. For it was then that one of the other lads voiced his disgust.

"I didn't like that policeman at the station," he said, bitterly. "He told me that I would never make it in the Navy!"

With that a chorus of seven or eight voices chipped in, "He told me that too!"

And everybody, including, and perhaps especially, Jackie, felt better.

On arriving at the naval training base, H.M.S. Raleigh, the new recruits were taken immediately to their sleeping quarters. Some of the lads gasped in horror as they were shown inside the old wooden huts, which had been there from the Second Word War.

The officer whose job it was to allocate them their bunks said, "Make sure you make the best of the summer, lads. These huts can be very cold in the winter."

When they had been given an hour to settle in, the recruits were brought to a large hall where a senior officer gave them all a talk on the honour, and the hardships, of being a member of the Royal Navy.

Jackie looked around the room and apart from his travelling companion from Ballymena, who had been assigned to a different division, was billeted in a different hut, and was already with different friends, he didn't know a soul. Not a single one.

At the end of his talk the officer held up a travel pass.

"I have a number of these available," he volunteered. "If anybody wants to go home, I will give him one. Just come up and speak to me afterwards. You would be better to go now and not waste time and money, if you are not going to stay, for good!"

It sounded tempting.

The living conditions were hardly four-star, the training promised to be tough, and he hadn't made any friends in his own division, yet...

But there were no Troubles over here, and the prospect of sailing serenely across endless shimmering blue seas under endless sunny blue skies was fantastic. And then there was Hong Kong. He really wanted to see Hong Kong...

So Paddy from Belfast made up his mind. He was staying.

A number of the lads couldn't face it, though. They took the officer up on his offer, picked up their passes, and departed.

But Jackie Dickey stayed. He wasn't giving in, or giving up, yet.

The training was tough, but Jackie could accept that. He hadn't expected a Sunday school picnic.

One of the aspects of life on H.M.S. Raleigh he had least expected to have to cope with, though, was the care of his uniform. At home Granny had always looked after his clothes. She had always maintained that household tasks such as washing and ironing, cooking or cleaning, were 'woman's work'.

Now he thought of her often as he was scrubbing his shirts on a washboard in a big tub in one of the huts. Granny used to scrub his shirts on a washboard in a big tub in the scullery, at home, or on a bright day in summer the whole washing operation was performed in the tiny back yard.

As the days went on Jackie made some friends and gradually became accustomed to the training schedule. After six weeks, though, he was dealt another blow, a double whammy.

Paddy from the South of Ireland couldn't take it any more and left the Navy, and in the same week, Paddy from Ballymena, whom he had travelled over with, decided the Navy was too timid, and transferred to the Royal

Marines. The only two other lads from Ireland in the entire training unit had left!

The biggest test of all came at the end of Part One of the course. Everyone was granted a long weekend off, to go home, but because of 'the Troubles' in Northern Ireland Jackie wasn't permitted to return to Belfast. Moore, a friendly Scot invited him to spend the weekend at his home in Glasgow but that wasn't allowed either.

So Jackie Dickey, the youngest apprentice at H.M.S. Raleigh, was forced to spend the long weekend on the base with a skeleton staff of officers and maintenance and catering personnel.

He was very, very lonely. And he was very, very homesick.

He had joined the Navy. But now he had lost any ambition he ever had to see the world.

Forget Hong Kong.

The only place he wanted to be that weekend was back in Belfast.

He just felt like packing it all in, like some of the rest of them, for good.

Had the sarcastic policeman been right after all?

Was Paddy not going to make it in the Navy?

Chapter Five

THAT'S AWFUL STUFF!

Jackie somehow survived the isolation of that terrible, testing weekend, and his friends, when they had heard of his lonely vigil, vowed they would never let it happen again. And they didn't.

'Paddy', as everyone called him, was the youngest member in the division and all the other lads rallied round to help him. Some of them even went so far as to organize a rota to take him home with them on weekends off.

In early December, with their training almost complete, the twenty lads who remained of Jackie's original class of forty were informed that before they went off on Christmas leave, they would be given their permanent postings. Everyone would be assigned to a ship to commence his Navy service, for real.

Now, suddenly, after all the rigours of the training and the homesick summer days, Jackie had two exciting events to anticipate.

He would be told of his posting, and then he was going to be permitted to go home to Northern Ireland for the first time since joining H.M.S. Raleigh, on Christmas leave.

When the day of the drafting came, Jackie was up early and had a shower. Then after the shower, when he was dressing in the uniform which he had gone to such pains to have perfect, he remembered Granny's advice. 'If you are in any sort of trouble, son, you can talk to God. Just say the Lord's Prayer.'

Although he wasn't really in trouble, Jackie did want to talk to God. He had something big, something very important on his mind, and he thought that maybe God could be of some assistance. The only problem was, though, that he didn't think the Lord's Prayer would state his case strongly enough. He would have to find some other form of words.

When he had checked that he was alone in the hut, Jackie decided that this was his moment to talk to God.

Dashing down on to one knee beside his bunk he said, at 'All this day Thy hand hath led me' speed, 'Please God, my Granny told me I could always talk to you. If there is any chance of it, please could I get on this new ship? Could I please be drafted on to H.M.S. Ariadne? Thank you, God. Amen.'

Then, with as much haste as he had bent down on to the one knee, Jackie jumped up off if, dusted that kneeling knee until it was the same navy as his other knee, and walked out of the hut.

He was on his way over to take his place in the line.

There was a buzz of excitement among the lads. All of them wanted to be posted on to the new ship, which was to be commissioned on March 1st 1973, H.M.S. Ariadne. Each of them knew, though, in his heart of hearts that not *all* of them would be drafted on to Ariadne. But they also knew that *some* of them would.

In the midst of all the excited chatter, when all the hopefuls assessed each others' chances, each usually rating his mate's probability much greater than his own, all of them inwardly, secretly, hoped that he would be one of 'the lucky ones'.

When it came Jackie's turn he was marched in before the Divisional Officer and stood to attention.

"Junior Seaman Dickey, what ship would you like to be drafted to? Do you have a preference?" the lieutenant enquired.

"Well, sir, I would love to go to H.M.S. Ariadne," was the Junior Seaman's immediate response. He had been asked a direct question, and so had given an honest answer.

The Divisional Officer shook his head slowly, and Jackie's heart sank quickly.

Then, still all proper and poker-faced, the lieutenant continued, "You will be pleased to learn then, Junior Seaman Dickey, that you have been granted your wish. You are being posted to H.M.S. Ariadne."

Jackie Dickey punched the air and yelled, "Yeoooooo!"

It was only then that the serious face of the sedate officer behind the shiny desk split into something resembling a smile.

This Division leader had seen a number of these passionate Paddies pass through H.M.S. Raleigh over the years, but he had never been able to figure them out completely!

When her sailor grandson arrived back in east Belfast for his Christmas leave, Granny was overjoyed to see him.

"And do you know, he's going to be sailing on a big new warship, too!" she would inform the neighbours with gusto tinged with gravity. Anyone listening to Granny would have thought that Junior Seaman Dickey, soon to be seventeen, was a kind of a Christopher Columbus, Francis Drake and Horatio Nelson all rolled into one!

Mary Gibb's only regret was that she couldn't see her latest hero in uniform. Jackie had been warned by his senior officers not to appear in uniform, back home in Northern Ireland, 'for security reasons'. So Granny had to be content with a box-Brownie photograph, which one of Jackie's pals had taken of him during the summer, and which he had kept carefully for her.

It was a tremendous thrill for the new sailor to join his new ship in early March 1973, after all the training and all the waiting. Jackie and his shipmates on Ariadne were the envy of some of the other lads who 'hadn't been so lucky.'

It wasn't all glitz and glamour, though. It was constant, and sometimes difficult work. Now all they had learnt had to be put into practice. And what was more, their newly commissioned ship had to undergo tough sea trials.

A welcome respite from the routine and rigours of their new posting was the shore leave. After the first set of trials Ariadne put into port for a weekend and her crew were allowed to go ashore in Weymouth. It was summer, and when the local and holidaymaking lasses discovered that these smart young lads who were swarming all over the place were in fact sailors on shore leave, they all just danced the nights away.

In mid-August, when all the sea trials had been complete, and the ship was back in Plymouth harbour, some of the more experienced sailors aboard began to send minor shock waves through the ranks of the novices, the juniors, the likes of Jackie and his mates.

The ship's company had been told that they were putting to sea in two days.

That sounded good to the juniors. Perhaps they were going to see some real action. And they might even begin to realize their dream, and see at least a bit, of the world.

Their youthful anticipation soon turned to niggling anxiety, however, when some of the 'old hands' began to whisper that 'this must be serious stuff', for live ammunition, both shells and missiles, had been brought on board.

There was only one way to dispel that lingering disquiet and that was to make the best use of their last two days leave. All the ship's crew were determined to go ashore and 'let their hair down', in one fantastic final fling.

Two nights before they were due to sail away on their, as yet unspecified, mission, almost the entire ship's company of H.M.S Ariadne descended upon the Pussy Cat Club in Plymouth. They pushed a number of tables together, tossed a heap of money into the centre, and began to drink.

And Junior Seaman Dickey, the youngest member of the group, was drinking nothing but Bass Shandy.

As the night progressed, and the drink flowed, heads became lighter and tongues became looser. It was then that Davy Cowan, who was Jackie's 'sea-dad', a kind of self-appointed mentor, said to his still sober charge, "Here, Paddy, take a drink of that!" and passed him across a Bacardi and Coke.

When Jackie lifted it up to his lips at first he stopped.

It smelt funny.

"Go on Paddy, drink it up!" some of the other lads coaxed. "That's a real man's drink!"

Having no desire to be counted 'a chicken', but rather wanting to be seen as a sailor lad doing what sailor lads did, Jackie drank it up, as urged.

When he had finished he put his glass down on the table, pulled a wry face and exclaimed, "Oh! That's awful stuff!"

His shipmates laughed.

"Don't worry, Paddy," Davy Cowan consoled. "The first and second drinks are usually hard to get down, but after that you develop a taste for it."

He then turned and called to a passing waitress, "Here, dear, bring us all another round of Bacardi and Coke!"

When she had brought a tray loaded with drink, a second glass of spirits was placed before Jackie 'Paddy' Dickey. And as the other men drank theirs, so he drank his, even though he still found the taste rather revolting.

Then he had another one.

And another.

And another...

Three hours later the seventeen-year old Junior Seaman was carried back aboard his ship.

He was full drunk.

When he woke up in his bunk the next morning the whole cabin seemed to be going round and round. And he felt he was going round with it! First he thought he was down on the floor, and then he thought he was up on the ceiling. Then he was sure he was just passing a porthole...

Jackie called out, startled.

"Help! Help! Something's happening to me!"

His shipmates laughed at him, again.

"There's nothing happening to you Paddy!" they crowed, barely able to contain their mirth. "All you have is a hangover!"

It took Jackie all the remainder of that day to work off his hangover, and he didn't have long to worry about it either.

For within twenty-four hours his ship had put to sea.

And it was only then that the ship's crew were told where they were going.

As soon as he heard of their assignment Jackie's dreams of shimmering seas in sunny climes all vanished overboard, like the constantly appearing, then disappearing, spray.

H.M.S. Ariadne was heading for the mountainous grey-green waves of the North Atlantic.

The 'Cod War' was then in full swing and she was steaming, fully armed and full speed ahead, for *Iceland*!

Chapter Six

FLOAT LIKE A BUTTERFLY

Despite many of the crew's initial reaction of 'Iceland!' or 'I thought we would be going to…' some of their late summer and early autumn patrols around the fishing grounds off Iceland turned out to be quite pleasant. And Jackie and his shipmates learnt a lot about the practical side of life on board a ship on active service.

As autumn advanced into winter, however, the weather became progressively worse, and life on board became a lot more unpleasant. It was then that the novices aboard Ariadne learnt a lot more about the less alluring aspects of Navy life on active service.

By mid-November they had an additional concern.

The crew had been informed that their next tour of duty, in 'the New Year', was to be to the Far East, and the promise of that had been helping to keep their hearts up during stormy days spent sailing heaving seas.

To Jackie the prospect of such a trip would just be a dream come true. He might even manage to see the mystical Hong Kong!

As the Cod War seemed no closer to a solution everyone aboard began to wonder if they were going to be forced to forfeit their trip to the sun just because a few men couldn't agree about a few fish.

It all worked out well for them, however.

A settlement was reached, the Cod War ended, and Ariadne was back in her home port of Plymouth just in time to allow her crew to disperse on Christmas leave.

It was on 6th January 1974, the newly promoted to Able Seaman Dickey's eighteenth birthday that H.M.S. Ariadne sailed out into the English Channel, on her way to the eagerly awaited tour of duty in the Far East.

This was it.

Jackie was off to see the world.

Their first port of call was Gibraltar and soon after they had tied up the sailors were allowed to go ashore. The more experienced seamen were anxious to show the new recruits two of, what they considered to be, the chief attractions of The Rock.

The first of these was a street where there was a bar every few hundred yards, and the other was the famous colony of monkeys.

On his initial trip ashore Jackie joined his companions as they began to 'drink their way along the street'. He wanted to show them that he was as much a man as any of them. Surely he was a 'hardened' sailor by now, having served on a warship for all of ten months!

Jackie never made it to the end of the street, though.

His friends had to half-carry half-trail him back to his bunk aboard, totally intoxicated, long before he reached it.

And it was two days later before he was fit to focus on a monkey.

After leaving Gibraltar one of their next ports of call was the Gulf State of Abu Dhabi, in the United Arab Emirates. Their stopover in that state was logged as a goodwill visit. The sailors didn't mind what it was called. The main thing was that it afforded them an excuse to go ashore and enjoy themselves! Their only problem was that since this was a goodwill visit by the British Navy the sailors were expected to wear their uniforms both on and off the ship.

And it was so hot! It was so very, very hot!

Some of the more mature members of the ship's company relished a visit to the U.A.E. for gold was cheap there, and they were able to buy their wives and girlfriends expensive looking charm bracelets at reasonable prices.

Since Jackie Dickey had neither a wife, a girlfriend, nor a superabundance of money, the opportunity to invest in the purchase of gold trinkets didn't excite him.

There was something else, though, which did.

One afternoon a few of the lads came back on board with some sensational news.

"Do you know what?" they told everybody they met, whether on not they were remotely interested. "Muhammad Ali is staying at the Hilton Hotel. And he puts on a show for the guests, and for visitors, in the bar every evening!"

That was enough for Jackie and a number of his friends who had been fans of the world champion boxer.

"That's where I'm going this evening boys," Davy Cowan announced. "Anybody game to come with me?"

There was a chorus of replies. And every one of them was a shouted, "Yes!"

When the scorching heat of the day had given way to the clammy heat of the night, a high-spirited group from H.M.S. Ariadne set out for the Hilton Hotel. There was Ginge, Oats, Phil, Paddy Comber, so called to distinguish him from the other Paddy in the party, Paddy Belfast, who was Able Seaman Dickey, and their sea-dad, Davy Cowan.

When they arrived into the crowded bar the giant of a boxer was already there, doing his party piece in a mock-up ring in the centre.

What struck Jackie immediately were the man's good looks. He had always imagined heavyweight boxers to be ugly, lumbering, hulks of humanity, with hopelessly scarred faces, puffy, evil eyes and cauliflower ears.

Muhammad Ali was more like a film star than a boxer. He was perfectly groomed, immaculately dressed, and breathtakingly handsome!

When the mighty monster model in the ring spotted the group from Ariadne in their distinctive uniforms he shouted down, "Hi, there! Are you lads British sailors?"

"Yes, we are!" came the response, in such perfect unison that it sounded rehearsed.

"Come up here, we want to see you," the Hilton's star attraction went on.

"All the nice girls love a sailor!" he quipped.

One by one Davy Cowan and his crowd trooped up through the admiring audience and then climbed and clambered into the ring, their exertions affording everyone an unexpected laugh.

Navy hats fell around the boxer's feet.

Muhammad picked Jackie's up and clapped it on his head. It looked so incongruous, such a small hat on such a big head, and yet the hat's proud owner thought it looked just great on its latest wearer.

The charming host began to ply the group of sailors with questions, which they answered, about where they had come from, where they were going to, and why they were there in Abu Dhabi.

When he was satisfied that he had spoken to each one of his guests individually, the boxer then invited a question from them.

"Is there anything you lads would like to ask me?" he said.

"Yes there is," Davy piped up. "Can we do your song and dance act with you?"

"Sure you can, man!" the born showman was delighted with such a request. "Now what you have to do first is learn the words. They are,

"My name in is Muhammad Ali,

I float like a butterfly,

And sting like a bee.'

Say them after me…"

And so they did, seven voices in chorus.

One leader and six learners chanted enthusiastically,

'My name is Muhammad Ali,

I float like a butterfly,

And sting like a bee…"

"That was good, lads! Very good!" their tutor encouraged. "Now all you have to learn are the actions!" And with that the towering figure started to dance around the ring, jabbing at each of his pupils with a mighty fist which knocked them off balance with the slightest of touches!

The sailor chorus performed their act four times to rousing encores, and when they had finished, with everyone breathless except the still immaculate boxer, a group of British tourists, who were staying in the hotel, rose to their feet spontaneously and applauded enthusiastically.

They thought these 'guys from home' were good!

Before they stepped out of the ring one of the lads asked Muhammad for his autograph, and he soon found that all his sailor fellow-showmen wanted it.

The great man was happy to sign all the autograph books, scraps of paper, napkins or beer-mats that were pushed at him.

It added to his image. Helped inflate his ego.

Jackie was so proud as he took his place with the others at a table in the bar. He had sung and sparred with a world-renowned boxing legend. And had his autograph in his pocket to prove it.

This was some night to remember. So he and his friends set about marking it in the only way they knew.

They drank, and drank, and drank. The laughter rang out, the pile of money in the middle of the table disappeared, and the Bacardi and Cokes disappeared too, one after another.

The liquor left Able Seaman Dickey floating, in his mind, like a butterfly...

But next morning it stung like a bee.

Back in his bunk he had yet another hopeless hangover.

Chapter Seven

POLE BEDS AND ELEPHANT LEAVES

Next port of call for Ariadne after Abu Dhabi was Hong Kong.

And Jackie realized a lifelong ambition! He was being permitted to visit that fabulous faraway place that he had often dreamed about in flights of fancy. As the ship steamed into the busy colony's busy harbour Jackie thought he had never seen anywhere so beautiful, in a majestic stately kind of way, in his life.

After a few weeks there, however, H.M.S. Ariadne sailed on to Singapore and since she was due to spend six weeks in port for a refit, her crew were stationed in barracks ashore.

This was a totally new experience for them. A lad even came in every day to make their beds, look after their laundry, and polish their boots.

This was what they had joined the Navy for!

Now they were seeing the world, and living it up as well!

After the first two weeks though, when the ship's company had seen all of Singapore they wanted to see, and sampled all of the local brew they needed to drink, they began to look for something different to do. And for Jackie Dickey that came in the form of the Army's School of Infantry Jungle Familiarisation course.

One day a poster advertising this course appeared on the notice board in their barracks and anyone wishing to be considered for it was invited to sign his name. Jackie was one of the first to pass the poster and when he read that the course lasted for eight days out of barracks, and that there was extra money for it, he was one of the first to sign 'the sheet below', to express an interest. It would always pass a bit of time, he thought, and earn him some extra money for some extra booze!

A few hours later the list on the board was full. Obviously more than Jackie had fancied a few days, 'away from it all'! When he saw that, and knowing there were only six places on the course, he decided that he wouldn't have a chance.

But he was wrong!

When the list of the six seamen chosen to represent H.M.S. Ariadne on the jungle survival course was posted up, two days later, the second name on it was Able Seaman Dickey!

Not knowing exactly how he felt about it at first, Jackie hunted out one of the other sailors who had been selected to go on the course and asked him, "Hey, Billy, I see you are going on this jungle thing, too. Have you any idea what it's all about?"

"To tell you the truth, Paddy, I haven't a clue! I just put my name down for a bit of a laugh!" came Billy's frank reply.

"That makes two of us!" Paddy Belfast laughed. At least he wasn't the only one who was totally oblivious to what lay just up ahead.

They were soon to find out, though.

Shortly after dawn on the first day of the Jungle Familiarisation Course Jackie and his five companions from the ship were taken by truck to the Army training base camp at Nee Som.

On arrival all the new recruits to the course were checked in and asked to give all watches and rings into the safe keeping of the camp commandant. Then they were all issued with their jungle kit, which comprised of two sets of camouflaged green uniform, one for the daily trek, the other for the nightly camp, a cumbersome kit bag containing everything that they might need, and a self-loading rifle, an SLR.

When the trainee jungle soldiers were told to 'kit up', which was another way of saying, 'Get all that stuff on!' the training officer bawled Jackie and one of his shipmates out.

"Are you two sailors?" he roared.

When a shameful nod of the head indicated that they were, he remarked, somewhat less aggressively, " I cannot understand it. For some reason or another you sailors never seem to be able to get the gear on right first time. Help them sergeant."

And a helpful sergeant did as commanded. He helped them sort all the belts, buckles and buttons into their correct places.

That was only step one, however!

The six men from Ariadne spent the next two days getting to know the others with whom they were to work very closely over the next week, in Nee Som training camp, under the eagle eye, and curt command, of crack SAS instructors.

They were taught how to use an SLR.

They were taught how to build pole beds.

They were taught how to survive in the jungle by hunting, trapping and fishing.

They were taught how to climb into, and out of, a helicopter, loaded down with a full jungle survival and combat kit. This operation had to be performed in double quick time under the baking sun.

'And be warned, your life could depend on how quickly you can do this!' they were told...

They were given malaria tablets and issued with a supply to take with them into the jungle. Precise instructions as to dosage were included in the pack.

'And be warned, when you are out in the jungle it is up to you to remember to take them as directed. If you should happen to forget you could come back a very sick man. That is, of course, if we consider you worth bringing back at all,' they were told...

The training was very demanding and if it hadn't been for one positive element many of the lads would never have completed it.

That single compensating factor was the sense of camaraderie, which developed amongst the participants.

One of the instructors told them on the first morning, that for the duration of the course, all the privileges and differences of rank would be forgotten. "The jungle," he explained, "is a mighty leveller. It is all for one, and one for all, out there."

And so for the introductory two days in Nee Som barracks, RAF pilots, Hong Kong policemen, British and Singapore Army officers, and the six selected sailors from H.M.S. Ariadne all mingled together, assisting each other.

Nobody knew where anyone else had come from except those in his own group. All each member of the group knew about any other member of the group was his Christian name, and that is how they all addressed each other.

On the second night, after their basic camp training had been completed and the toughening trainees were preparing to head out into 'the real jungle' next day, Jackie remarked to Tom, "If it wasn't for all the fun with all the other lads, I don't think I could take this. When I think of what I left to come here! I had three good meals a day, my bed made every morning, and my boots cleaned every night. I must be daft or something!"

Tom laughed.

"Cheer up Paddy! Keep your chin up!" he urged. "You will make it no problem!"

Jackie was encouraged, and concluded that Tom must not be related in any way to the Plymouth policeman of his earlier training days!

It was next day, when all the men on the course abseiled out of a hovering helicopter, to meet the training team, already there, in what seemed to Jackie the heart of the jungle at the far end of nowhere, that they were expected to put all their training-to-date to the test.

Their initial task was to build temporary shelters, in which to spend that night, out of forest materials. These were constructed from branches of trees and roofed with elephant leaves, which were huge leaves of a forest plant. Within that shelter each man built his own pole bed consisting of two trimmed poles, which the bed-maker had to find and prepare himself, criss-crossed, for a mattress, with the stems of tough climbing plants called lianas.

Each succeeding day after that brought with it a new experience, each one, it seemed, more laborious, or more loathsome, than that of the day before.

Their exercise on one of the first days was on map reading, finding their way about in the jungle.

Another day it was on first aid, and community relations. The party were marched through a village of jungle tribes-people and their task was to make friends with the natives, without the important tool of a commonly understood language. This they were taught to achieve by a series of gesticulations, and generous donations of sweets and trinkets all around.

By the third or fourth day most of the group members were adapting fairly well to the privations of jungle survival, although the total prohibition of cigarettes during training frustrated some of Jackie's fellow participants. But it was the prohibition of all alcoholic drinks that bothered him. There wasn't a beer or a Bacardi, a rum or a vodka, to be seen, or drunk!

No one was allowed to carry money with him either, but not many cared about that. They didn't pass many department stores on their daily excursions!

On one of the days the team had to wade, almost shoulder deep across a fast-flowing river. The problem in this case was that every man was carrying a pack, which it was his duty to keep dry. This they were taught to accomplish by wrapping all their gear up in the versatile, and waterproof, elephant leaves.

Paddy Jackie found the trapping and killing of the wild animals for food the most difficult thing of all. When they thought their charges were sufficiently prepared for it the instructors set them the task of killing and skinning a goat, and then cutting it up and cooking it. The plaintive cries of that animal as the inexperienced, but inexpressibly hungry, butchers endeavoured to kill it, lived with Jackie Dickey for days...

Eventually the course was completed, the party returned to Nee Som barracks where each man was presented with a certificate confirming that he had successfully completed a 'Jungle Familiarisation Course in Malaysia.'

Then, after some emotional partings, for the group members had come to know each other well and respect each other a lot, during the eight days of the course, they all returned to their units, scattered across southeast Asia.

As his party was being driven back to the naval barracks, which had become their home, Jackie reflected on the course, and realized that he had actually enjoyed it. This in a measure surprised him, for he had by then come to believe that he needed to be continually drinking alcohol for enjoyment. Yet because he had been busily engaged in other more pressing pursuits, like learning how to stay alive, he had survived a week drinking only water from a flask clipped to his belt!

On arriving back at barracks, though, all prohibitions were forgotten about, and Jackie and the other five embarked upon a 'Happy Hour' of eating, drinking and making merry, which actually lasted for three days!

As other somewhat envious members of the ship's company called in on the revellers to enquire how they had fared, it gave Jackie and the others great pleasure to recount some of their experiences in graphic, and occasionally conveniently exaggerated terms.

Able Seaman Dickey was growing up fast.

Although he didn't realize it at the time, either, the weapons training of Nee Som camp, and the survival training of the Malaysian jungle could also prove beneficial in years to come.

Chapter Eight

WELL DONE, SAILOR!

The next four years in the life of Jackie Dickey were spent in a routine and non-too-taxing round of sailing the seven seas. He and his shipmates sailed from port to port where they invariably drank themselves senseless ashore.

Jackie was fulfilling his ambition to see the world, but after the first flush of excitement there soon came a monotonous sameness, a peculiar emptiness about it all.

Yes, he was now 'one of the lads', a smoking, swearing, virtual alcoholic. But deep down, though he never admitted it to anybody, he was not completely satisfied.

He was seeing the world, sure enough, but there must be something, somewhere, which he was missing. For some vital, and as yet inexplicable, ingredient was lacking in his life.

Jackie's six-year term in the Navy ended on July 6, 1978, and soon after his discharge and return to his native Belfast, he signed up to join the Ulster Defence Regiment. The Troubles were then in their most violent years, with people being maimed or murdered almost every day, or so it appeared to the returning son of the city. Since his Navy service had endued a sense of patriotism within him, Jackie considered membership of the U.D.R. as an opportunity to further serve his country.

In mid-August, with only slightly more than four weeks ashore behind him, Jackie was summoned to attend a one-week training course in Ballykinlar Army Camp in County Down. By this time ex-Able Seaman Dickey was twenty-two years old, and as he looked around at all the eighteen year olds lined up beside him on the training-ground he thought they looked like little more than schoolboys.

He was an experienced seaman and it wasn't long until he discovered that some of these raw recruits looked up to him as some sort of returning hero, and because of his Navy service they all immediately nicknamed him 'Sailor'.

On the second day of the course the drill sergeant produced an awesome looking weapon and asked the group of wide-eyed, open-mouthed, soon-to-be-soldiers, "Has anyone here ever used an SLR before?"

Jackie Dickey was the only one who even knew what the letters SLR meant, and thus the only one in a position to answer that question.

"I have, sir," he volunteered.

"Then you can help me with the weapons training for these others and you will act as their escort when out on patrol, Sailor," the sergeant announced.

It wasn't long, either, until Sailor was called upon to put his weapons training into practice. After the course he was posted, with 7th Ulster Defence Regiment to the army base in Belfast's Grand Central Hotel, just a few hundred yards from where he had worked as a lad in the offices of the 'Belfast Telegraph'.

During the autumn and winter of 1978 and into the spring of the following year, Jackie was mainly posted on duty to the security gates at Donegall Place, just across from the City Hall. And there, on each shift, he worked in conjunction with a regular soldier.

It was the soldier's duty to search all the males passing through the gates into the city centre, whilst specially appointed women searched all the passing females.

Jackie Dickey's duty was to stand guard over all of them with his SLR.

Nine days out of ten everything carried on as normal, or as normal as things can possibly carry on with every individual passing into the shopping precincts having to be stopped and searched. City people had become accustomed to this, acutely aware that the ultimate object of the exercise was their own personal safety.

There were the occasions, though, when things could be different, and even dangerous.

One such time occurred in June 1979.

It was a beautiful, sunny, mid-summer morning. A steady stream of shoppers in light summer clothes and light summer spirits passed steadily in through the security gates, but although the passing public had no hint of it, the guards on the gates were being extra vigilant.

At their early morning briefing before coming out on duty they had been warned to be especially alert, for intelligence units suspected that there would be 'a hit' on one of the city centre gates that day.

It was well that Jackie and those on duty with him on the gate had taken heed of the tip-off, for just after mid-morning when Jackie was beginning to consider the pleasant prospect of an hour off for lunch, the 'hit' happened.

A line of people were standing waiting patiently to be admitted, one by one, through the security gates and Jackie was standing at the kerbside, watching all around. Both training and experience had taught him to be ever watchful, always wary, for you never knew who was going to attack you, or when, or where.

Suddenly a white car came racing across past the front of the city hall, being driven at speed, its horn blaring, against the flow of traffic.

Jackie sprang into an action position at once. He cocked his weapon and prepared to shoot, but couldn't since there were so many civilians in his line of sight.

There followed a sharp crack! crack! crack!.. as a machinegun was fired repeatedly from the back window of the speeding vehicle. The gunmen, though, must have realized that they couldn't single out their intended targets, Sailor and his soldiers, without injuring innocent civilians, either, for they shot nine or ten times into the air before roaring off, causing consternation to the approaching traffic.

It was a warning. We have been here, and don't worry, we will be back, it said. And next time, too, we won't miss!

As he was stepping back when the car had gone, Jackie heard a sigh, then there was a rustle followed by gasps from a number of those waiting to pass through the checkpoint.

A wee ginger-haired security woman in her fifties who had been standing behind Jackie fainted at his feet!

There was general confusion for a moment or two until a glass of water was produced from a nearby shop, and when the lady was well enough she was helped in there for a rest.

Fully aware that he was still carrying a loaded weapon Jackie asked a number of people to stand aside until he made it safe. He was afraid of an accident in such a crowded street.

The patient people waiting to pass through the gates appeared totally unperturbed by the whole situation, however. Jackie was unsure whether to smile broadly or bawl loudly when he heard one man say to another, "Tell me Sammy, what's that fella making all the fuss about?"

Shots had just passed over their heads, a woman had collapsed on the street, the man in front of them was carrying a primed and loaded gun, and they were wondering what all the fuss was about!

When Jackie arrived back into the Grand Central Hotel base for lunch, his fame had gone before him.

The wee woman who had fainted had been taken back there in a Land Rover to recover from her ordeal, and she obviously thought that at least half the shots she had heard had come from Jackie's gun. She honestly believed that Sailor had made a heroic and single- handed assault on terrorism. At least that was what she was telling everybody!

So impressive had she been in singing the praise of this hitherto unsung hero that when Jackie Dickey entered the mess it was to a chorus of, "Well done, Sailor! You are a brave man, Sailor!"

Sailor tried his best to convince them that he was not a brave man at all.

He tried to explain to them that he had not even so much as fired a single shot! There hadn't been a chance to do that!

It was, however, all in vain!

Nobody listened to him. He was just being extremely modest they thought, in addition to being extremely brave.

At last he gave up and just revelled in the adulation.

And later that evening, when he came off duty, he would enjoy the little gift his fainting friend had left him, just as a token of appreciation to the one who had so bravely risked his life to save hers, as she thought!

It was the last thing Jackie Sailor Dickey needed, though!

For it was a bottle of vodka!

Chapter Nine

SITTING DUCKS

Monday, August 27, 1979, was one of the darkest days of the Troubles up until that point, for it was on that day that the seventy-nine year old Earl Louis Mountbatten was killed, along with three others in his boat in County Sligo, and then eighteen soldiers died in two successive bomb blasts near Warrenpoint, County Down.

In the wake of these atrocities the security forces began to fear that the Provisional I.R.A. would consider that they were beginning to gain an advantage in the continuing conflict, and launch further attacks. In an attempt to thwart such strikes the Army decided to increase 'the number of men on the ground', and also the frequency of the patrols. It was their intention to 'saturate the Border counties', from where, it seemed, these attacks were most likely to be launched.

As part of this increased security presence, Jackie's Company, 7th U.D.R. who were then based in Palace Barracks, Holywood, were posted to South Armagh, in September.

They were airlifted by helicopter from Palace Barracks to Gough Barracks in the city of Armagh, from where they were then transported in a variety of military vehicles to a number of separate secret destinations, which were different every time they went out.

Each of these patrols lasted for three or four days in open country. The soldiers were all armed with SLR' s and dressed in camouflage combat kit. They snatched whatever sleep it was possible to snatch, lying below a hedge or in a potato field, with members of the group taking it in turns to keep a round-the-clock watch.

In an attempt to lure the would-be assailants from cover a group of three or four soldiers from each patrol would go on foot-patrol through open country, backed up by a hidden ambush team. Since the soldiers acting as decoys were in effect little more than 'sitting ducks', men were not commanded to undertake this dangerous exercise, but rather volunteered to do so. Such was the sense of loyalty amongst the members of every patrol, however, that when someone volunteered to take part in such risky manoeuvre, then everyone volunteered.

They all took turns to lay their lives on the line.

The days seemed endless on those patrols.

And the weird, eerie stillness of the night was even worse.

It was simply petrifying.

The men spoke very little to each other when out on those terrifying anti-terrorist patrols.

The tension often became almost unbearable.

No one ever laughed.

There was no levity of any sort.

Each man was usually totally engrossed in his own thoughts, and inwardly selfishly engaged in his own fight for survival, both physical and mental.

Will this be my last trip? Jackie often asked himself, crammed into the back of an Army truck alongside twenty or so other men, each of whom was asking himself that selfsame question.

It was tough.

Tensions were high.

Morale was low.

Sudden, violent, unexpected death was a distinct possibility.

At least, Sailor Dickey had tried to console himself, during his first tour of duty 'on the ground' in south Armagh, when they all returned to their base camp in Palace Barracks, out of the immediate danger zone, after their spell on duty, everybody would feel free to relax, laugh, and enjoy themselves for a day or two.

He was soon to discover that it didn't work that way, however.

When they arrived back to base, with all the restrictions on smoking and alcohol left behind for perhaps a week in the lonely, leafy lanes and farmer's fields they had been patrolling, there was no immediate explosion of relief.

Still very few of the men spoke to each other about anything of any significance.

The silence was sinister.

One of the first things the returning patrol found on a number of occasions was the display of photographs. On the walls of the mess there would be hanging a newly framed photograph, or perhaps even more than one newly framed photograph.

These photographs were of soldiers, many of whom had been firm friends of the men coming back. And beside the photograph, or photographs, would be a neatly typed notice of the soldier's name, rank and number, and nearby there would be a series of newspaper cuttings in all shapes and sizes explaining why that particular soldier hadn't made it back from some particular sortie. Why his portrait was in that bizarre picture gallery.

They could have been shot by a sniper or bombed to bits.

And they were only the men who had been killed.

When the off-duty patrols recovered sufficiently to want to talk to anybody they would find out from the men stationed in Palace Barracks about some of the others, the survivors, 'the lucky ones'. These were the men who hadn't lost their lives. They had just lost their arms, their legs, or their eyesight.

In order to allow these sullen, shocked soldiers to return to something resembling normality, the camp authorities had decreed that whenever a patrol returned from a tour of active service, whether in the middle of the day or the middle of the night, it didn't matter, the bar in the mess was to remain open until either the mess ran out of drink, or the men ran out of money.

There were two sure signs that the strain amongst the mixed-up men in the mess was easing.

The first was that they began to talk. Gradually a buzz of strangely frantic conversation increased in crescendo.

And the second sign was that they began to fight. The pent-up aggression, which they had been prepared to use on the enemy, was taken out on each other. These were never serious, malicious fights. They rather just signified the awaited explosion of tension.

A few hours later the mess would be closed down again, and silence would descend.

The soldiers would all have resorted to the relative comfort of their bunks.

The 'sitting ducks' would almost all be dead drunk.

Chapter Ten

ALL WIRED UP

The mess was full, and the men were just beginning to wind down and open up.

They were just approaching the twitchy talking, petty squabbling stage.

It was a Sunday night and Jackie's unit of the U.D.R. had just returned from a period of duty on the County Fermanagh border, where they had been stationed in St. Angelo barracks, near Enniskillen.

Northern Ireland was by then passing through another period of increased unrest. It was late November of 1980, and by then the I.R.A. hunger strikes had polarized people even further, if that were possible.

Members of the security forces who were constantly in the front line of all hostilities, felt extremely vulnerable. And for Sailor Dickey and his fellow-soldiers in 7th U.D.R. border patrols in County Fermanagh had differed little from border patrols in County Armagh.

There had been the same endless edginess.

There had been the same long, sullen, sombre, self-reflecting silences.

There had been the same inbuilt but unspoken terror of the sickening thud of a sniper's bullet in the chest, or the deafening roar of a trip-wire detonated booby-trap bomb.

This was their chance to relax, and put it all behind them, at least for a while.

As they sat around the tables talking one of the lads announced that Jim, another member of the regiment, had just been issued with a new personal protection weapon, which the men referred to, for convenience, as a PPW.

That gave Jackie an idea, or perhaps rather it afforded him the chance to implement an idea he had been contemplating for the previous six months, at least.

When he was sure that nobody would notice, or think it strange, he left his chair and went over and sat down on an empty one, across from Jim.

After some pretty pointless chat, Jackie broached the subject.

"I say, Jim, I believe you have been issued with a new PPW," he began, nonchalantly.

"Aye, that's right," came the reply, as Jim replaced his glass on the table after a swig.

"Any chance of having a look at it a minute, Jim?" Jackie went on to enquire.

"Why Sailor? Why do you want to see it? Sure it is just the same as everybody else's. You have probably one the same yourself for that matter." Jim was puzzled.

"You are probably right, Jim," Jackie conceded. "But I don't carry one, and I would just like to see yours, if that's O.K."

A few drinks had helped Jim shed his inhibitions, and since Sailor was one of their most experienced soldiers, what could be the harm in showing him his shiny new gun? Having convinced himself that nobody would mind, Jim reached down into the pocket of his combat trousers and sliding the gun across the table, under his hand, said with the air of someone doing his friend a fantastic favour, "There you go, Sailor."

Jackie lifted the pistol and examined it closely. This was unusual behaviour for somebody who worked with guns every day. There was, though, an ulterior motive behind his abnormal curiosity as he fondled the loaded weapon.

Gently, almost reverently, he placed it back on the table, and this time it was his turn to conceal it with his hand.

Now all that remained for him to do was await his opportunity.

He hadn't long to wait, either, for it came about ten minutes later.

Jim had gone up to the bar to order another round of drinks, and the three other men at the table were engaged in an argument about the music and merits of some pop group or other.

Sliding the PPW off the table Jackie shoved it hastily into his own pocket, and then shouted across, above the din, "While you boys are yelling at each other, I'm away to the toilet!"

Nobody took any notice.

With men who were downing so much drink, the toilet was the second most popular location in the mess, next only to the bar.

Sailor Dickey found an empty cubicle and locked himself in.

He knew what he was intending to do.

The pressure had become too much to bear any longer.

He was totally convinced that one of these days he was going to be shot by the 'Provos'. So why should he not deprive them of that pleasure and shoot himself?

One bullet in the brain would end it all.

Then he wouldn't have to worry about anything, any more.

When he had done it they would hear the crack, break down the door, and bury him with all the rest.

He probably wouldn't get his picture on the wall, but that wouldn't really matter...

Jackie Dickey sat for a few moments staring down the barrel of the gun. It was loaded and primed, ready to fire. Gradually, and with a hand that was beginning to shake, he brought it forward and placed the point of the barrel between his eyes, just above his nose.

It felt cold, and hard. But at least with the forward pressure on his forehead he could hold it steady there.

No, he decided.

I can't do it like that.

He then moved it around and pressed it against the right side of his head. Now he could feel it, but not see it.

And when he pressed the trigger that would be the last he would have to see or feel of this pointless life...

At that moment, sitting on a toilet seat in a locked cubicle, with a loaded gun boring into the side of his head, Jackie fell into a trance. Incidents from his earlier days flooded across his mind. His boyhood days, selling lemonade, Alex, Granny, sunny days and seasick nights in the Navy, horrible days and horrendous nights on patrol, the fruitless futility and unceasing uncertainty of it all...

Suddenly he was jolted out of his reverie and back to his senses.

Somebody was shouting at the top of his voice, "Where are you, Sailor? Are you all right? What are you doing in there all this time, anyway?"

Jackie recognized the voice at once.

It was his best mate, 'Stewartie'.

"Don't worry, I'm O.K." Jackie yelled back, hastily clearing the gun, and returning it to his trouser pocket.

"Well then you had better get out here fast!" Stewartie went on. "Somebody has reported Jim's PPW missing and the C.O. (Commanding Officer) has come down and is kicking up a real racket!"

Before they returned to the mess, Stewartie said, "Here Sailor, give me the weapon." And he held out his hand.

Jackie handed it over, sheepishly, shamefacedly, like a schoolboy who had just been caught on pinching a couple of Polos from somebody else's packet.

"What are you going to do with it?" Jackie wanted to know, when he saw Stewartie tuck it inside his tunic.

"You'll see, Sailor," he replied with a twinkle in his eye. "Or maybe even you won't!"

As they re-entered the mess, mayhem met them.

The C.O. was bellowing, "Close the bar! Close the bar!"

Men were scuttling about searching every shelf, and some were even crawling about, scouring the floor.

Suddenly someone raised a triumphant shout, "Here it is!"

Jackie and Stewartie had joined the ever-so concerned searchers, but what Jackie didn't realize was that part of Stewartie's search had been to plant the gun in a not too obvious, but not too obscure position, at the back of the mess where somebody was bound to find it sometime.

With the recovery of the PPW, everybody heaved a sigh of relief. Losing a gun was a dangerous thing, and could prove fatal if it were to find its way into an enemy's hands. But now that the mysteriously missing gun had been traced, the bar was reopened, and everybody celebrated the restored calm, by having another drink.

As they were walking back to their billets together, later that evening, Jackie said to his friend, "Thanks for your help there this evening, Stewartie. If you hadn't come in to the toilets when you did, dear knows what might have happened."

Stewartie tramped on in silence for a few minutes, thinking.

Then when he had considered how best to put it, he offered the grateful Jackie some sound advice.

"Don't let anybody know you are thinking of doing yourself in, Sailor," he counselled, gently informing his mate that he had a fair idea what he had been contemplating.

"For if you do," he continued, an impish smile dancing around the corners of his mouth, "they will send you over to Musgrave Hospital to one of them English headshrinkers, and do you know what they do to you over there? They wire you all up to an electric current 'til your hair stands on end and your eyes pop out!"

Jackie laughed, briefly. It was a short, shallow laugh, but the first time he had laughed in days.

Although he suspected that Stewartie's description was rather exaggerated, he had no desire to be all wired up, to that extreme.

For he was all wired up already.

His nerves were at breaking point.

And sometime, somehow, something was going to have to snap.

Chapter Eleven

A POINTLESS LIFE, OR A KITCHEN KNIFE?

The continuing pressures of life on constant patrol drove Jackie Dickey to depend even more on his sole safety valve. Alcohol.

And within the next two years he became a total alcoholic.

His addiction became so bad that in May 1982, he left the U.D.R. He had to.

Although he was not forced to resign from the regiment, Jackie chose to. For his own and everyone else's safety.

There were occasions when he found himself setting out on patrol, in charge of a deadly weapon, half drunk.

And in his few sober, sensible moments he recognised that this was totally unsafe.

On being demobbed Jackie applied for, and was appointed to, a job in the Belfast shipyard of Harland & Wolff, whose giant cranes dominated the skyline where he had been brought up. The 'Yard', as the locals called it, had been a part of Jackie Dickey from childhood. He was back to life in 'Civvy Street', and back to live in Frome Street, but not back to the same house as he had left.

Since Granny Gibb had died in 1979, Jackie went to live with his aunt Mina and uncle Jack in their house just a few doors up from where he had spent his carefree teenage.

For another two years Jackie spent all week working in the ship repair section of the shipyard, and all weekend spending all the money he had earned all week, in the Harland & Wolff Welder's Club in Dee Street.

It became an established pattern for the ex-sailor, ex-soldier, ex-sensible citizen.

You worked all week, and drank all weekend. Every week, and every weekend.

In April 1984, uncle Jack and aunt Mina's twenty-three year old grandson, Mark, had a serious road accident, and for days his life hung in the balance. During those difficult will he, or won't he, make it days, Jackie was left on his own in the house, for his uncle and aunt spent most of their time, both day and night, in the Ulster Hospital, Dundonald, at, or near, the critically ill young man's bedside.

On Saturday night Jackie staggered home alone from the Welder's Club.

He had bought, and brought out with him a forty-ounce bottle of Blue Vodka. That would pass the night for him, he thought.

When he entered the silent house Jackie poked the feeble fire which had almost gone out in his absence, threw a few lumps of coal on it by hand, from the scuttle by the hearth, pulled a chair up in front of it, and sat there.

As tiny fingers of orange-red flame began to splutter out from below and around the black lumps in the grate, Jackie came to thinking again about the meaningless nature of life, as he knew it.

Slowly he drank a glass of vodka.

Then slowly he smoked a cigarette.

And always he tried to discover a convincing reason to prolong this agony.

But couldn't.

I am twenty-eight years old, he told himself, and I have seen the world. Now I am stuck in this aimless, pointless routine.

What is the point of anything? Is there *any* point in anything, any way?

The shiny wooden clock on the mantelpiece had just struck midnight, when Jackie answered his own question, to his own satisfaction.

There was no point in anything, so there was no point in continuing.

Rising unsteadily from his chair he stumbled into the kitchen and dragged open the top drawer in a set of cupboards below the tiny bench on which aunt Mina had for years performed all kinds of culinary miracles. For Jackie knew that it was in that top drawer she kept her kitchen knife, which was sharp as a razor.

He rattled through the weird collection of wooden and metal, stirring and mixing, cutting and mashing utensils, until he found the knife he wanted.

Then, after pulling it out he stumbled even more unsteadily back into the living room, leaving the drawer hanging open.

Now it was time to finish it all.

And he would do it this time, for good.

Settling back into his chair before the fire, he slowly sipped another glass of blue vodka.

And then he slowly smoked another cigarette.

What he was going to do was the only answer to his misery. He thought. But it would take a lot of inebriated courage to perform. He knew.

When he had thrown the butt of his most recent cigarette into the fire where it disappeared into one of the last flickering flames, Jackie took the kitchen knife in his right hand and laid the blade flat across his left wrist. A twist of the blade and then a little pressure applied would sever an artery. And if he had enough strength when he had that done he would somehow slash his right wrist as well.

He knew the blade was sharp. So he thought it wouldn't take long…

But he had to think about it.

As he sat in that chair before the fire that was already beginning to die into a heap of silent, fluffy, grey-white ash, he glanced up at the picture above the fireplace.

Since he had lived in that house now for years, Jackie had seen that picture thousands of times. And he had often gazed at it before.

The picture was a print of a head and shoulders painting of a beautiful dark-skinned girl with sparkling eyes. The girl in the portrait was wearing a pale blue dress which showed off, by contrast, her smooth, shining skin, and around her head she had wrapped material in the same colour, to form a headdress. This was fastened at the front with an elaborate jewel-studded brooch.

In idle, envious moments Jackie had stood staring at the picture and wondering why it was that he had never been able to see girls like that on his way to work or in the Welder's Club.

Tonight though, it was different.

As soon as he glanced up at the familiar picture, his eyes were arrested by it. He couldn't stop gaping at it. Jackie tried to shake himself out of his stupor and the flat blade of the knife made itself felt against his wrist. Then he rubbed his eyes.

For in the frame, he saw, not the foreign girl in blue, but the face of granny Gibb, gazing gently back down at him. There she was, her face creased by age and care, her bun neat except for the few stray hairs that had always insisted in trying to make their escape. The white collar of the blouse she often wore below her black dress stuck up as it had always done, starched and stiff.

Jackie sat motionless, mesmerised.

Was he dreaming? Or was he hallucinating?

What was happening to him?

He didn't know, and his mind was so befuddled that he couldn't even be bothered to try to figure it out...

The early light of an April morning was beginning to peep in around the corners of the curtains when Jackie Dickey stirred again.

It was after six in the morning.

The room was cold.

Granny had disappeared and the girl in blue had claimed her rightful place back in the picture on the chimney breast.

A kitchen knife lay against the hearth, the tip of the blade pointing into the flameless, smokeless, lifeless fireplace.

An empty cigarette packet lay half opened on the floor, where Jackie had dropped it.

An empty vodka bottle lay on its side at his feet. He must have kicked it in the night.

A glass with half an inch of vodka still left in it sat, still loyally upright, on the floor by his right hand where he had left it down to pick up the knife...

And Jackie Dickey was still alive.

His life had been spared.

Again.

Chapter Twelve

WHAT SHALL WE DO WITH THE DRUNKEN SAILOR?

After that night of the knife, and the brush with death, Jackie Dickey felt ill.

He was so sick during the day that he was unable to go to work.

And he was so scared during the night that he was unable to go to sleep. As he lay in bed Jackie found himself afraid even to close his eyes, for every time he did he had horrendous hallucinations. Fantastic fiends, emissaries of evil, dragons of death, besieged his tormented mind.

At the end of a worried, workless week, Jackie dragged himself along to the Harland & Wolff Welders' Club on the Friday night. He reckoned that if he could 'get full' again it would put him out of his misery for another miserable day or two.

As he sat around a table with some of his regular boozing partners, one of them, Sammy, looked across at him and said, "Hi Sailor, we are going on a holiday to Spain in July and one of the boys has dropped out…"

Before Sammy had even time to finish his sentence Jackie jumped in. "Can I go?" he enquired eagerly, seeing opening before him another escape hatch from his currently harrowing experiences. And this time it would be for two weeks!

Sammy looked over at the other two lads at the table who had already arranged to go on the trip.

"What do you think, boys, should we let Sailor come?" he asked them.

They both nodded limply and one of them replied, little more than half-heartedly, "Aye, I suppose so."

Turning his attention back to Jackie, who was awaiting their decision, Sammy summarised it for him.

"O.K. Sailor, you can come with us, but strictly on one condition," he announced, with the air of somebody laying down the law.

"And what's that?" Jackie asked, having a fair idea what it might be.

"It is that you don't get drunk and disorderly and get us all chucked out of Spain!" came the emphatic reply.

"Thanks, fellas," Jackie said, genuinely grateful for the opportunity they were affording him. This would always be something to which he could look forward. Then a cloud crossed the horizon of his thinking. There was another matter he hadn't as yet taken into account.

It would be better to air it sooner rather than later.

"Only problem is, boys," he went on, "at this moment in time I have no money. Not a bean."

It was a big, but not insurmountable, problem.

"Tell you what, Sailor," Sammy was prepared to settle for a compromise. "If you can raise the money inside four weeks you can come with us. But you must promise to behave yourself!"

Jackie went home that night feeling better than he had done for weeks, for now he had something upon which to focus his mixed-up mind.

He wasn't drunk.

He couldn't afford to get drunk in front of those boys!

They would kick him out of their sunshine party straight away!

Later that night, after he had told his aunt and uncle about the prospect of a summer holiday in the sun, but the immediate shortage of the required sum, uncle Jack came to the rescue.

"I'll lend you the money, Jackie, provided you can pay it back to me before you go," he volunteered.

That was great. Jackie promised he would, and he did.

On the following Monday morning Jackie returned to work impelled by a new motive, and applied for every hour of overtime available. Then for the next couple of months he worked all week, and every weekend too, in ship repair, in order to repay uncle Jack, and to have a reserve of spending money for his holiday.

The amazing thing was, also, that Jackie Dickey, whose alcoholic habits were a watchword in the neighbourhood, kept off the drink for three months!

He couldn't afford it, for he needed every penny he could save, and he kept telling himself that this abstinence would prove good practice for a temperance trip to Spain!

When the day to which they had all looked forward for so long eventually arrived and Sammy, Sailor, and the other two set off on their holiday, the three who had been somewhat apprehensive about inviting 'Sailor' Jackie to join them, could scarcely believe it.

Sailor wasn't drinking!

This was fantastic! He must have taken to heart all that he had been told. Incredible!

As soon as they arrived at their apartment in Santa Ponsa they all made a quick change of clothing and set out in the pursuit of pleasure. That was what they had saved for, and that was what they had come all this way for, so there was no time to waste.

Jackie felt all pleased with himself. He changed into his new white T-shirt, and with two thousand pesetas pushed into the back pocket of his new white shorts, he was set to make this one memorable holiday.

Before launching themselves upon the attractions of the town the four friends decided to have a few drinks at the bar in the apartment block to celebrate their safe arrival in sunny Majorca. And Jackie thought he had been teetotal too long. Now that he was on holiday surely there could be no harm in having a beer or two with the boys?

There may not have been, or so he thought, but it wasn't long until the craved after can of beer was not enough.

Sailor had sailed the seven seas, and Sailor was a seasoned drinker, or so he thought.

And it wasn't long until he was parting with his pesetas at a rapid rate, and knocking back the vodkas one by one.

As they left the apartment to find out what the town had to offer in the way of pubs and clubs, Jackie, who was already tipsy, assured his friends, "Now don't you boys be worrying about me. I wont get drunk or do anything stupid or anything like that you know!"

Sammy & Co. were not so sure about that, though.

And their worst fears were soon to prove well founded.

For when their white-robed friend began drinking bottle after bottle of the local wine in a nightclub they knew what was coming, and withdrew to another table.

About an hour later the other three lads, who were still sober, were sickened at the sight of what was happening before them.

Jackie, who had given so many pledges, and seemed to be keeping so many promises, was on the other side of the room, full drunk.

His despairing minders crossed to him and shouted, "Hi Sailor, we are going across to Magaluf. Are you coming?"

"Aye sure boys, I'm coming!" Sailor shouted back, rising shakily to his feet and trying valiantly to stand up straight on unsteady legs.

This was just exactly what his friends had feared.

This was just what Sailor had been warned about so often. But he was their friend, so they thought it their duty to try to help him.

With their steadying arms around him and strong shoulders to lean upon the staggering Sailor make it to the outskirts of Santa Ponsa.

But from there he could go no further.

And his three companions were fast running out of strength, of time, and of patience.

To make matters worse Jackie had fought them away when they were trying to direct him, and then had stumbled out into the road where he had collapsed, totally inebriated, and unable to move.

Car horns began honking as angry motorists had to drive around this senseless, powerless, specimen of humanity, lying in the carriageway.

Sammy and the other two risked their own lives to try to lift him, but found they couldn't.

A curious crowd was beginning to gather.

Soon the police would arrive and the longsuffering lads who had brought this drunken sailor to Majorca figured that if they were caught in his company they would all be sent home.

So they decided to make themselves scarce.

This wasn't an all out, full scale, taking to their heels and running like the hammers, desertion, but rather a knowing nodding in the direction of Magaluf, and a discreet disappearance into the crowd.

And they were away.

Sailor Dickey was on his own, so drunk that he could neither rise, stand, or walk. He lay abandoned in the middle of a busy road, between two buzzing holiday resorts.

Some holiday strollers, enjoying the balmy warmth of the late summer evening joined the curious crowd on the kerb.

Others peeled away from the crowd, and passed on, shaking their heads and muttering something about 'mad Irishmen.'

But nobody moved either a finger or a foot to help him.

Although in a drunken stupor, Jackie somehow realized the gravity of his situation, and began to panic.

He was a sorry sight, and barely recognizable as the smart young holidaymaker who had left his apartment some hours before.

His clothes were in a mess.

His mind was in a whirl.

His legs felt half-solid and half-liquid like a half-set jelly.

And he couldn't possibly get up. There was just no way he could rise, or move, or help himself.

He lay there, a spectacle to all. But nobody came to his aid.

Soon one of these honking cars with their swearing drivers would hit him and that would be it. Curtains. The end. Full stop. He would then be finished with this futile life at last. It would be a messy way to go, and not the one he would have chosen, but it seemed that now he had little choice...

Suddenly, in spite of himself, and stiff with terror, Jackie Dickey cried out in absolute agony of mind and soul, "O God, please God! If there is a God out there, please help me now!"

Then his head sank down upon his arm, pressing it into the stones of the road, and he heard a voice, which seemed so soft and soothing, so caring and so comforting, wafting to him as though on a warm and gentle wind, and saying, "I love you. I died for you. I will help you..."

Sailor lay there stunned, but strangely stilled.

Was he hearing things? Or hallucinating again?

Could that be true?

Would his panic prayer be answered?

Or would the next bus hit him and squash him flat?

Chapter Thirteen

LORD, SAVE ME!

When Jackie Dickey next surfaced in consciousness he was in a police station in Magaluf. And he was in a sorry state. His once white outfit was now spattered with tar and stained and stinking with sick. His head throbbed as though about to burst.

A policeman came forward and offered him a glass of water, and encouraged him to drink it. Jackie did, but it tasted funny.

Half an hour later, a tall blonde girl in short shorts and with an admirable all-over tan came into the cell where he was being held.

Although he was still feeling absolutely awful, this attractive girl attracted Jackie's attention straight away. She was just the kind of girl he and his mates had hoped to meet to help enhance their holiday. He knew that he was hardly likely to make a big impression on her in his present state and condition, however!

Within a few moments Jackie began to realize why he had been honoured by a visit from this lovely young woman. She was an interpreter whose job it was to try and make sense out of this senseless Irishman.

"What's your name?" she asked him.

"Jackie," Jackie replied.

"Jackie who?" the girl went on.

"I don't know," Jackie replied.

"Where are you staying?" the girl interpreter persevered.

"I don't know," Jackie replied.

"Well who are you with?" the girl tried another tack.

"I don't know," Jackie replied.

It wasn't that Sailor was being either unreasonable or uncooperative, he just found himself unable to either think straight or remember anything. So much drink in such a short space of time, had left him with a totally muddled mind, and a temporary loss of memory.

The go-between had just shaken her head in despondent frustration, and was turning to leave when sorry Sailor made his first somewhat sensible suggestion since being lifted.

"If I could see the lads I was with I would know them, I'm sure!" he claimed.

Big help that was, on a crowded holiday island!

Where would Jackie, who didn't know where he was, go to look for his three friends who would by now be lying low to avoid deportation for having been seen with him?!

Jackie spent a miserable, sleepless night in stuffy police cell, sweltering in the stench of his still smelly clothes, which were stuck to him with sweat.

The only relief in the drawn out distress of the long night hours was the regular visit of yet another duty policeman with yet another drink of water. The station officers were used to coping with such situations, and knew they couldn't allow this dismal drunk to become dehydrated.

Next day, when Jackie was beginning to talk more sense the policemen put him in the back of their patrol car as they cruised from Magaluf to Santa Ponsa and back. If he ever saw his friends he was to let the driver know.

The morning proved fruitless.

Jackie had thought it would. The three of them would have been out for most of the night before, and so would probably have been asleep for most of that morning.

As the day wore on, and became hotter, Jackie who was still feeling wretched, suffered a setback in his return to normality.

He developed 'the shakes'. His arms, legs and body began to tremble uncontrollably.

It was in mid-afternoon that Jackie, who felt cold in spite of the heat, and dark inside despite the bright sunny day, saw his three friends.

Sammy and the other two were sitting, chatting and laughing, at a table in a street café, just about two hundred yards from their apartment block.

"There they are!" he croaked, instinctively. "That's my mates over there!"

The driver stopped the car, and Jackie tried to get out.

When his feet hit the ground he began to shake all over like a leaf on a tree in a stiff breeze. He leaned against the car to steady himself.

What a pathetic sight he looked.

"Hi boys! Come here!" he shouted across to the three at the table.

On seeing the police car draw up, and then Jackie lurch out of it, his companions were about to beat a hasty retreat when the only police officer who knew a smattering of English called out, "It will be all right! You are not in any trouble!"

That was welcome news!

So they came slouching back to be rewarded with the sad spectacle and sickening smell of their friend Sailor.

"Can you take him back to where you are staying?" the policeman asked Sammy.

"Yes. Never worry, we will take care of him," Sammy replied, hugely relieved to be allowed to remain in Santa Ponsa.

When they arrived back to the apartment Jackie peeled off all his sweaty sick-stained stinking clothes and put them in a plastic bag and tied the neck of it. He never wanted to see them again!

He then proceeded to have a welcome shower.

As he was drying himself, one of the other lads, not keen to miss all that precious sunshine outside, said, "We will give you an hour to get yourself sorted out, Sailor. Then we will be back for you. We are all going out tonight. That is, of course, as long as you don't get full again!" With that parting shot the outside door banged, and they were away.

Although he had just finished drying himself, Jackie should have felt all clean and fresh, but he didn't. So he went straight back into the shower.

Then, having towelled himself down for a second time, and with his hair at the still wet and sticking out stage, he went and had a look in the mirror.

What a scary image met his gaze!

A pale, gaunt, grey-green face stared back at him out of wild, frightened eyes! And to make matters worse, the monster in the mirror had a two-day growth of beard!

"I will have to shave!" Jackie determined. "I can't possibly go out with the lads looking like that!"

What he had forgotten, though, was that half-drunk men with hollow-feeling arms and shaking hands shouldn't be using safety razors!

For by the time he had finished, his face resembled something laid out on a butcher's block. He had cut himself in a dozen places. Spots and streaks of blood, in all shades from bright red to a deep, almost black, maroon, had formed a crazy pattern on his cheeks and chin.

When the others came back to collect him to take him out for the evening, Jackie hadn't helped his appearance. They discovered him lying on top of his bed with tiny fragments of torn-off toilet paper stuck to his weird selection of self-inflicted cuts, to stop the blood.

Sammy laughed out loud when he saw him.

Sailor's face looked like a picture of a map he had seen once in a book about the War. It had been a map with little pinned paper flags peppered all over it to show the position of planes.

"Right Sailor, are you ready?" he enquired, trying to recover a straight face.

"No, lads. I'm not going out with you, tonight. You go wherever you want. I feel awful!" Jackie told them.

None of them had the heart, or the cheek, to tell him that he looked awful, as well.

They took him at his word, though, and set out for a spree, leaving Jackie to contemplate the prospect of another night of lonely misery.

After being left alone Jackie lay motionless on the bed for a while, hands cupped behind his head, staring into space. Was there not anything more to life than this? he wondered.

An hour later, when 'the shakes' had abated sufficiently to allow him to grasp and hold objects almost steady, Jackie swung his legs over the edge of the bed, and bending down, slid his case from below it.

What he was intending to do, he wasn't quite sure, but he felt compelled to open his case. Perhaps another change of clothes would help his mood.

As he rummaged through the case, and all the items he had bought and brought, Jackie discovered, tucked into the left hand front corner, something he hadn't known was there.

It was a Gideon New Testament.

Uncle Jack had offered to lend his nephew his case for his holiday, but Jackie didn't know that it came complete with complimentary New Testament. And wherever Uncle Jack had got it from, Jackie could never quite fathom, for he certainly wasn't a New Testament type.

Nonetheless, Jackie pulled it out and began to leaf through its pages. They were stiff and fresh and had not been often opened.

In a strange way, Jackie felt glad to have found that little book.

There might be something in it worth reading, and anyway he could always amuse himself trying to find some of the verses he had learnt in the B.B.

It was going to be a long night, and he wasn't going out anywhere with his toilet-paper mask on.

Slowly, silently, gradually, Jackie became engrossed in the book in his hand.

He stopped at pages and read bits. And then moved on again, stopping at other pages, to read other bits.

Suddenly he was startled by a verse that seemed to shoot off the page to meet him. It was not one with which he was extremely familiar, but he vaguely remembered having heard it somewhere before, perhaps the B.B., or perhaps the Salvation Army in Dee Street.

It was Ephesians chapter two, and verse eight.

Jackie read it over, and over, and over again...

'For by grace are ye saved through faith; and that not of yourselves: it is the gift of God.'

That was what he needed, he knew. To be saved through faith. But how did you become saved through faith? It wasn't from or by himself, it was, it said, 'the gift of God'.

Jackie now not only knew that he needed to be saved, but he also wanted to be saved.

And he knew, too, what he needed to do.

But he hadn't a clue how to do it.

He needed to pray to God, and ask God to save him.

But he didn't know what to say.

He didn't speak the language.

Then he remembered Granny Gibbs advice, of fully fifteen years before. 'Son, if you are ever in trouble, you can talk to God. Just say the Lord's Prayer'.

Slipping off the bed onto knees that were now shaking for a totally different reason, Jackie began repeating in a soft whisper, 'Our Father which art in heaven, hallowed be Thy name. Thy kingdom come...'

When he had finished the prayer he knew off by heart, Jackie Dickey stayed on his knees. A sense of longing for God, a craving to be closer to his 'Father in heaven', had overtaken him.

He buried his head in the bedcovers, and remained motionless.

Spread-eagled there, half kneeling, half prostrate across the bed, verses he had learnt in the B.B. Bible Class and the Salvation Army Sunday School all came flooding back. They were all in the New Testament, which had fallen on to the floor beside him, but Jackie didn't need the little book that had started him off on this train of thought, now.

One by one he remembered them...

'For God so loved the world that he gave his only begotten Son, that whosoever believeth in him should not perish, but have everlasting life'...

'I am the way, the truth and the life: no man cometh unto the Father, but by me'...

'Come unto me, all ye that labour and are heavy laden, and I will give you rest'...

Suddenly he raised his head, and cried out in anguish, "O God help me! Please do something for me! I need you and I believe in you, O God! Please Lord, save me!"

Then Jackie fell down across the bed again, weak, exhausted, but surprisingly, and supremely, content.

It was only then that Jackie realized how desperately tired he was. He felt like falling asleep, but he rose, changed and slid into the bed.

As he lay there, just before sleep overtook him, Jackie Dickey was overwhelmed by an unusual sense of calm. It just flowed and floated over him, like the voice on the road had done, the night before. All the panic had gone. A deep-seated peace that was hard to explain had taken control of his whole being.

He felt as though God, his Father in heaven, had made a special journey down to where he lay, just to tuck him into bed, and bid him 'Good-night'.

And in that absolute assurance that all was well between himself and God, Jackie drifted off into the soundest sleep he had experienced for months.

Perhaps even for years.

Chapter Fourteen

THE BEST HOLIDAY WE EVER HAD!

The peace of the night before extended to become the peace of the next morning, as well.

When Jackie awoke to greet the new day he felt like a new man.

It was just after seven o'clock and yet he wanted to be up, to be out, to be doing things. For the first time in years he actually wanted to live.

And on a more earthly, practical, personal plane, he was hungry.

Jackie slipped out of bed quietly so as not to disturb the other three who must have returned to the apartment at some stage during the night. They were all fast asleep, their clothes strewn amongst the empty beer cans littering the floor.

Picking his steps carefully through this obstacle course, he made his way across to their fridge. How he would dearly love something to eat!

The fridge was full, crammed full, indeed so full that there would not have been room to put anything else in it. But although this was a self-catering apartment, the fridge was full, not of food, but of drink!

Self-catering for Sammy, Sailor & Co. had meant catering for themselves with as much booze as they could afford. Stocking up with food was, to them, something that women did at weekends, but had never crossed their minds as being any part of their holiday!

A dramatic change seemed to have occurred in the basic desires of Jackie Dickey, however. For now all that drink didn't appeal to him in the slightest. He wanted something to eat!

Pulling on a clean pair of shorts and his sandals this 'new creation' left his room-mates to sleep off the night before undisturbed, and made his way downstairs.

When he discovered that the breakfast bar was already open he bought himself a bacon sandwich and a mug of tea, and went outside to sit by the pool.

It was still barely seven-thirty, and Jackie was on his own, alone with his thoughts.

As he sat there, relishing food for the first time in days, he felt so happy. The warmth of the early morning sun warmed his body, just as the glow of new life in Christ warmed his soul.

It was good to be alive.

He was at peace with God and the world.

The still waters of the pool reflected the sunlight on to his face. He blinked in the glare, then turned round to face the full orb of the sun, the mug of tea dangling loosely in his hand.

His heart was bubbling over with a newly found joy.

"Thank you, Lord! Thank you!" he whispered, closing his eyes in an impulsive action of reverent satisfaction. And he kept them closed for a few minutes, allowing the heat of the sun, the still freshness of the morning, and the sense of being so close to God that he could almost touch Him, to wash over him in waves.

When he felt it was time to open his eyes again, Jackie looked all around him. It was funny, for everything seemed different now. He was seeing things, but particularly people in a new light.

As the holidaymakers from the apartment block began to dribble down to breakfast, Jackie realized that he was now, somehow, in some specific inexplicable sense, different from them.

His casual observations of the people around, and his personal reflections as to his relationship to them, led him to a sudden, and startling, recognition.

The boys upstairs, his mates, what was he going to do about them?

It was frightening at first.

What would they say?

They would think he had gone daft!

Telling them was going to be a problem!

But now he had Someone with whom he could share his problems.

Hadn't Granny Gibb always said, 'Son, if you are ever in trouble, you can talk to God'?

It had been sound advice, and 'Son' had used it before to good effect. Now, and especially after the previous night's experience, he was really beginning to get the hang of it.

When he talked to God, though, he talked to God. And that was it. He hadn't yet learnt how to go all the way around the world in a series of hackneyed phrases and bits out of hymns before arriving at the point.

So he decided to ask the Lord for help, and for guidance. It came as a kind of second nature for this newly born son in the faith to speak in intimate terms to his loving, caring, powerful Father, seeking his counsel.

Sitting there in his chair by the pool Jackie gazed up into heaven and said, or perhaps it was prayed, earnestly, "Lord, I have a couple of questions to ask You.

First of all, tell me this, How am I going to tell these mates of mine that You have saved me? I think the people in the churches call it 'born again', or something like that. I mean, what will I say to them, Lord?

And my second problem is, Lord, How am I going to finish this holiday with these fellas? I don't want to be going round like a Holy Joe spoiling their holiday, and yet I don't want to drink any more booze with them. What do You think I should do?

Thank You so much for saving me last night, and now I am looking to You for Your help. Amen."

Having aired his concerns, and made his requests, to the Lord, Jackie rose confidently from his sunny seat by the pool and went back up to the apartment. As it seemed that most of the other people in the block had by then made an appearance, in varying degrees of wakefulness, he was sure his friends should at least be stirring, if not already up.

They had all struggled out of bed before he arrived in their room and were at the stage of struggling to come to terms with another day.

Jackie greeted them all cheerily.

"Morning, lads!" he called. "If you boys want to go down to grab yourselves something to eat, I will tidy up this mess. Then when you come back up, I have something to tell you."

All three of them regarded him with slight suspicion.

Sailor was usually last to be up. But today he was by far the first.

And the mess had never seemed to bother him before. In fact he had been one of the best at making it. But now, today, it seemed to be getting to him.

It was too early in the morning to ask questions, however, and if Sailor felt like tidying up their singularly untidy apartment all the more power to him. If that's how he wanted to start his day, why not let him?

And they slunk sleepily down the stairs.

Jackie's big problem, though, was that they didn't come back up, as he had hoped they would.

Having dumped all the cans and bottles in the bin, tidied the beds, and sorted and returned all the scattered clothes to the top of the case of their respective owner, he waited. And waited. And waited.

But nobody came.

After almost an hour he realized that they had no intention of coming back up. They had probably found a seat in the sun, with congenial company, and forgotten that Sailor even existed.

So if they weren't coming to him, Jackie recognized that he had only one option. He would have to go to them.

For he just had to tell them what had happened to him, the night before.

Making his second trip down stairs that morning, the new convert prayed another of his frank and fervent prayers.

"This is it, Lord. I'm going to tell Sammy and the boys as soon as I get a chance here. So when I open my mouth, please will You tell me what to say? Thank You Lord, I know You will. Amen."

When he arrived down at the poolside Jackie scanned around and soon spotted his friends. They were sitting with two others, smoking and laughing, doubtless recounting the episodes and exploits of the night before. Every man had a bottle of beer before him.

The pool area had become busy and noisy by that time. At least a dozen children and teenagers had begun shouting and splashing in the water.

This was not the sort of place where Jackie had imagined he would first tell others of his faith in Christ. It would have been so cosy, so intimate, and so personal in the apartment with only his pals about, but that was not how, it seemed, it was going to be.

One of the lads saw Jackie as he dodged bodies and bathrobes on his way across to them.

"Hi Sailor! Come on over and join us! Where have you been? Have you painted the whole place and all?" he joked gently.

Jackie trailed a vacant chair across, and pulled himself into a position by the table, and waited. He would have to choose his moment carefully, and it wasn't long before it came.

One of the two to whom the other three were talking, a young man from the Irish Republic, turned to him and asked a point blank question.

"And what did you do with yourself last night, Sailor?" he enquired.

That was Sailor Jackie's chance.

The Lord had opened the door. Now it was up to him to go through it.

"To tell you the truth I wasn't out of the bedroom last night," he began, "for I felt so rotten and looked such a mess, that I just didn't feel like going out."

There was no response to that opener from any of the five lounging around the table, so Jackie cleared his throat nervously, and went on, "But I have to tell you what happened to me all the same. I don't want you to think I'm mad or anything, for I'm not, but I'm a Christian now. I was born again last night."

That bold declaration was met with a stunned silence.

Nobody laughed, as Jackie had feared they would.

Nobody jeered, as Jackie had feared they would.

There was nothing. No reaction. Just the stupefied silence.

Jackie was glad he had told them. He was glad to 'have it off his chest'. Now, at least they knew where he stood.

But how he wished somebody would say something. Anything even. Anything would be better than nothing.

Eventually, and to Jackie's profound relief, Sammy broke the silence.

Setting his beer bottle back on the table, he wiped his mouth with the back of his wrist before asking, incredulously, the question Sailor had told them not to ask, but which he had always anticipated.

"Sailor, have you lost your head?"

"No, I tell you I haven't Sammy," Jackie replied. "I mean what I said. I am a Christian now."

"Forget it Sailor," one of the other chaps advised. "Away up there and buy yourself a beer."

"No, I won't," was Jackie's response to that suggestion. "And what's more, I won't be buying any more beers. I am finished with alcohol, for good."

That one raised a few eyebrows.

Sailor, who once claimed that he could drink them all under the table, finished with alcohol. And 'for good'?

They would see. Time would tell.

Now that he had conquered the first hurdle, with the help of the Lord, Jackie now only had the second one to face.

How was he going to finish this holiday with this crowd?

And that evening proved his first big test.

"Come on Sailor, we are going to a disco," one of his friends invited and informed him, all in the one sentence.

Jackie agreed to go with them, for he didn't want to appear a stuffed shirt spoilsport. But what was he going to do?

When the other three had gone out of the apartment to their first stop, the bar in the block, Jackie remained behind, telling them he would be down 'in a minute'.

What his friends could never have guessed was that Jackie wanted that minute to talk to the Lord, and solicit His help and guidance. And before the left the bedroom he knelt down by his bed and said the Lord's Prayer. He was keeping in touch with heaven, his new home base.

That night at the disco Jackie did his best to allow his friends to enjoy themselves as they best understood how. And he drank only Coke. Gallons of it he felt!

One of the first he drank tasted peculiar.

He suspected something sinister.

"Some of you boys have spiked my drink!" he exclaimed. "That tastes of vodka!"

He was sure that one or all of them had hatched some sort of plot to bring him clattering down from his high and holy ideals.

The friends were flabbergasted.

"We didn't Sailor! It's as honest, we never touched it!" they all avowed, one by one.

And they were telling the truth.

Jackie Dickey was to discover that since he had been such an alcoholic it would be years before Coke tasted like Coke again to him. But it did, eventually.

Next day after the disco Jackie hired a car and for the rest of the holiday he took his friends different places, and they had a wonderful, relaxed, carefree time. They went go-kart racing, sightseeing, and visiting every town and village on the island.

And what Jackie didn't realize was that every completed day was an even bigger miracle to his friends. For they had been taking bets on how long this 'good-living thing' would last with Sailor.

Some had said two days, some had said three, but nobody, not one of them, had bet on the end of the holiday!

But they were every one proved wrong.

As they were standing waiting for their cases to come round on the carousel at Dublin airport, on their homeward journey, Sammy acted as spokesman for the others when he said, sincerely, "Thanks very much, Sailor. That was the best holiday we ever had!"

Jackie, in turn thanked him for that kind remark

It had been his best ever holiday, too.

But for a totally different reason!

Chapter Fifteen

A WEE PHASE

Returning home from a happy holiday, wonderfully refreshed and completely changed, was one thing. But telling Jack and Mina all about it in their house in Frome Street was another.

This would be his first big test back in Belfast. And his second call to stand up, stand up for Jesus, in an apathetic, or perhaps even unsympathetic, situation.

When he had unpacked his case and presented Mina with a pile of dirty washing and the souvenir gift he had brought home for his uncle and her, Jackie knew he would have a lot of questions to answer. Jack and Mina had been waiting eagerly for his homecoming for the last few days, and could hardly contain themselves, anxious to savour every detail of Sailor's stay in the sun.

"I have something exciting to tell you about my holiday," the new convert began, nervous anticipation of their reaction restraining him from either looking or sounding excited. "Something wonderful happened to me out there!"

"Great!" Mina exclaimed. "What happened? Did you meet a nice wee girl? Are you getting married or something?"

"No, Mina," Jackie went on patiently. "I didn't meet a nice wee girl, as you talk about, but I got saved. I let Jesus into my heart and He has changed my life."

Jack and Mina were both dumbfounded.

"And what exactly does that mean, Sailor?" Jack asked his nephew, when he had overcome the initial shock.

"It means that I'm a Christian now and I won't be smoking or drinking any more. And I won't be going to the Welder's Club or the 'Con' Club any more either."

"What you are telling us is that you won't be coming down to The Welder's for a drink with us tonight then," Mina said. After Jackie's totally unexpected declaration she found herself at a loss to know how to respond.

"Yes, that's right," Jackie repeated, softly, and with a smile. "You two go on as usual, but I won't be going."

Later that evening, just before they went out, uncle Jack spoke to his nephew again. Just to make sure he hadn't been mistaken in what he had understood earlier.

"Sure, Sailor, you are not coming with us?" he enquired.

"Yes, I'm sure Jack. I'm not going with you," Jackie reaffirmed his position once more.

Ten minutes later, after Mina had come down, all dressed up for her evening out, Jackie heard her say to her husband in the hall, as they were opening the front door, "He'll be back with us in a week or two. This is just a wee phase he is passing through."

The door slammed shut and they were gone.

And Jackie was left alone with his Lord.

He had barely been an hour on his own, however, when there was a rap at the door. On opening it Jackie discovered three of his former drinking friends, clustered around the step.

"Did you have a good time on your holiday, Sailor?" We all missed you over at the Club. Are you coming round with us for a drink?" one of them asked, breezily.

"No, I'm not , boys," Jackie began to explain it all again. "I am a Christian now and I won't be going to the club any more."

His three mates all regarded him strangely.

Had the holiday in the sun been too much for Sailor? Had he gone off his head, or what? Was this really Jackie Dickey talking?

"And when did this happen?" one of them asked, completely bewildered.

"In Majorca. You asked me if I had a good holiday. Well, I had, for one night out there I just asked God to come into my life and change it, and He did," their friend replied. "And I meant what I said. I have no desire to go back to the Club again."

"O.K. Sailor. We will leave you today, " another said. "But we will call back in a weeks or two's time. You will probably be over this by then."

As they turned away to set out on their night's socializing, Sailor called after them, "You needn't bother you know, boys. We can still be the best of friends, but I won't be going back to the Welder's again."

Thus ended another friendship. Other than meeting them on the street or in 'The Yard' where they all worked, Jackie seldom saw those lads again.

Although the Lord had given his new child in the faith both the courage and the opportunity to witness to his guardians, and his erstwhile boozing buddies, it annoyed him slightly that nobody seemed to be taking him seriously. One would think by their response that he had either thrown a childish tantrum or was recovering from a bad dose of the flu! Did nobody believe that an Almighty God could work an amazing change in his life?

Perhaps they would when they saw what he was determined to do in the coming week. The first thing that he had to do to show them that he meant business, was to cancel his membership of the two local clubs for he had no interest whatsoever in returning to either of them, and another was to pay off all his drinking debts.

Uncle Jack was enlisted to help him out.

The following weekend, after his next pay-packet, Jackie presented his uncle with his two membership cards and three ten pound notes. One of these cards was for the Harland and Wolff Welder's Club and the other for the East Belfast Constitutional Club, or 'The Con Club' as the members called it.

"Here Jack," the now non-drinking nephew began to instruct his uncle. "I want you to return my membership cards to both of the clubs. And that money you have there is to pay off my bills in both places."

His uncle eyed him curiously.

"Do you really mean it Sailor?" he enquired, beginning to think that maybe this was more than just a wee phase after all. Sailor seemed so certain about what he wanted to do.

"Yes. I want you to do it," Jackie repeated.

And within two days uncle Jack had done as requested, and Sailor, who had once been a legend for his love of the liquor in both clubs was no longer a member of either.

There was one outstanding debt, however, that Jackie Dickey was determined to settle himself. And that was to his father.

For most of a year previously Jackie had been borrowing drinking money from his father, who also drank a lot himself. When he counted it up Jackie realized that he owed him forty pounds!

He had been working overtime in the ship repair yard on a Saturday afternoon, and on his way home he decided to seek his father out. And he knew where to find him.

Father worked on the coal boats, and most of the dockers from the coal quays, both Protestant and Catholic, did their drinking in The Rising Tide Bar. It was common ground for both communities.

Jackie approached the bar somewhat nervously. He had never been back in a pub since that memorable night in Majorca, but he felt he had to see his father himself. He had to tell him the news, and pay him his debts, in person.

Since it was a Saturday, the place was packed.

When he opened the door Jackie was surprised at his reaction to the smoky, beery atmosphere. He didn't want to go in.

Fortunately, he didn't have to.

At a table half way up the bar he spotted his two brothers, Alex and Jim, who also worked on the coal quays, and who were also loyal patrons of The Rising Tide.

"Where's me da?" Jackie yelled at them, above the clink of glasses and the hubbub of conversation.

"Over there!" Jim bawled back above the din, pointing to a table down in the corner, and not far from where Jackie was standing, as he did so.

It wasn't long until father was on his feet. He had recognized both the voices.

"You want me Jackie?" he asked his son, directing him out the door again.

"Yes, I do, father," Jackie went on. "I want to talk to you"

"Well, we can talk out here in the hallway. You shouldn't be in there, son", his father replied.

So he must have heard!

Something else that happened in The Rising Tide on a Saturday was that there was an enterprising local barber who came into the hallway to cut the men's hair, reckoning that if the men were too busy boozing to come to him then he would go to them! And there were two chairs free beside each other, in the barber's stopgap salon.

"We will sit down over there," Alex Dickey senior suggested to his son, and immediately put his proposal into practice by stepping across and sitting down on one of them.

When Jackie had taken his place beside the older man, he outlined the purpose of his visit.

"I have come to tell you, father, that when I was out in Majorca on holiday I trusted Christ as my Saviour, if you know what that means. I became a Christian in other words," he explained.

"Yes, I've heard, Jackie, and I'm glad," was his father's instant reply. "That's the right thing to do."

"And there's another thing, too," Jackie continued. "I owe you forty quid, and I've come to pay off my debt". And with that he handed his father the money he owed.

They talked on for a few minutes in the busy bar entrance and makeshift barber shop, and then Jackie rose to go.

"I will go on now, father," he volunteered. "And that will let you get back to your mates."

"Thanks for calling, son, and for telling me that good news," the big burly man replied. "And here."

It was then his turn to push something into his son's hand.

"You will probably need that more than I do," he said. "And I believe you, too, Jackie. You have made the right decision. And I know you will live up to it."

As Jackie walked round home to Frome Street, it was almost tea-time, and he was hungry. But he was happy, as well, for a number of reasons.

He had been in a bar, and had felt no need for a drink.

When he took time to look at what it was that his father had placed in his hand he discovered that he had given him twenty pounds back. He had halved the debt with his son.

And at last he had found someone, his father, who believed both what he had to say and what he could do, or what God could do with him.

That was the most thrilling thing of all.

Chapter Sixteen

SURE THE LORD DOESN'T NEED TO KNOW!

Down at 'The Yard' Jackie Dickey worked in the office of the ship repair section. And Jackie's office had for years been an accepted rendezvous for all smokers, drinkers and gamblers, especially on a Monday morning with 'all the boys' anxious to outdo 'all the other boys' with the tales of their boozing and betting exploits of the weekend.

And it was on a Monday morning that the saved Sailor returned to his work. He knew that he was going to have to tell this crowd that he was now a Christian, and he was also acutely aware that it would not be one of the easiest things he had ever done.

On his way to work he prayed for help from God, and then devised a plan to break the news in the shipyard. It wasn't an easy way out of the situation, but it was what he considered to be a more comfortable way into it.

He would tell a sympathetic soul, and he had no doubt that such a soul would soon spread it around!

There was one man in the Yard whom Jackie knew to be a Christian, for this man, Pete Atkinson, had often spoken to him discreetly about his need to be saved. Indeed he had often told Jackie, who found it both amusing and surprising, that he and some others were praying for him.

It stood to sense that he should tell Pete first. If he had been as concerned about Jackie as he claimed to be, at least he wouldn't laugh at the new convert's confession.

He should, in fact, be pleased.

When he had opened up the office and attended to anything urgent, Jackie left his post and walked over to the machine shop where Pete worked. He was exploding with the news, and would have to tell Pete, or somebody soon.

The machinist didn't hear Jackie coming at first, with the noise in the shop, but when the man from the office in ship repair stepped up beside him, Pete greeted him warmly.

"Morning, Sailor. What can I do for you today?" he wanted to know.

"You can't do anything for me just at the moment, Pete," Jackie began. "But I have something I would like to tell you."

"And what's that?" Pete went on to enquire, with a sneaking feeling that it was good news, if the glow on Jackie's face was anything to go by.

"I wanted to tell you, Pete, that when I was on holidays in Spain there for a couple of weeks with some of my mates, I came to know Jesus as my Saviour!" Jackie burst out in a torrent, barely drawing breath.

"Praise the Lord! Praise the Lord!" Pete Atkinson exclaimed at the top of his voice, in an effort to be heard above the deafening din all around him.

Then, switching off his machine for a few moments, he turned to Jackie, his face aglow now, too.

"That's wonderful news! Tell me all about it, Sailor," he urged.

Jackie had been right in his prediction. He had come to the proper person. Pete appeared pleased.

And for the next five minutes he treated the captivated Christian to an outline of events in Majorca, including the police cell, the bedroom conversion, and the incredible change.

When Jackie had finished Pete threw his arm lightly around his shoulders and gave him a piece of interesting information followed by a warm invitation.

"You probably never realized it Sailor, but we have been praying for you for years down in our lunchtime prayer meeting and Bible Study group. And what you have just told me is an answer to our prayers. It would be great if you could come to our wee group down here today at half-past twelve. You would enjoy it," he told him.

The bit about boys from 'The Yard' praying for him for years came with a new meaning to Jackie at that moment. Pete had told him about it before but he had shrugged it off then as a sort of religious nonsense by a crowd of religious 'nuts'.

Now he was grateful to believe it. He was amazed, though, at the persistence of his praying workmates and the wonderful grace of God. For there had been a time when he was sure that nobody in the world cared the slightest iota about a drunken rascal like him.

The invitation to the lunchtime study group was one he felt he couldn't refuse. For one thing it would allow him to meet others of like mind, and it would also give him the chance to nail his colours to the mast of the good ship, 'Christian'.

So he promised Pete he would go.

Then he returned to his office, and to his work.

But it was going to be anything but a run-of-the-mill Monday morning.

Jackie was only back in his office about half-an-hour when Pete returned with two other men from the Study group. He hadn't been able to wait until lunchtime to share the fabulous news with his praying friends, and they in turn couldn't wait until his promised appearance at the Bible Study to meet their newest member. They insisted in seeing him straightaway so that they could all rejoice together.

The tidings spread around The Yard like wildfire.

It was on everyone's lips.

And they weren't all just as excited about the news as Pete and his praying pals had been, either.

Jackie's three most recent visitors were on their way out the door, still in euphoric praise to God, when they met Big Matt on the way in. He was a giant of a man, six foot four and burly with it, and he brushed the Hallelujah Chorus to the one side as he stomped past.

This was what Jackie had feared. And this was one of the characters whom he had asked the Lord, in one of his many prayer times about the matter, to help him with. For one of the jobs Jackie had undertaken in his office was to collect and sort out the Bingo cards from the Sun newspaper, every Monday morning. And he had determined that he would not be doing that any more, either.

Big Matt was one of his regular customers.

And Big Matt was a big man!

"Here Sailor, what's all this about you turning good living?" he wanted to know immediately, going straight to the point.

Matt wasn't one to mess about. And you didn't mess about with him, either.

"What you are hearing is probably right, Matt," Jackie proceeded to let him know, frankly. "I turned to the Lord on my holidays. I am a Christian now."

"And where does that leave us with the Bingo cards?" the big man roared on. Jackie could see that he was obviously panicking about his weekly 'flutter' and took some consolation from the fact that his bluster seemed to stem more from frustration than anger.

"It leaves us that I won't be doing the cards any longer, Matt," he told him.

"That's just what I thought you would say!" Matt wailed.

"Why can you not just keep on doing the cards, Sailor?" he implored.

Jackie felt sorry for him. But he had made up his mind, and could answer that question.

"I can't do the Bingo any more, Matt, for the Lord wouldn't like it," he told the baffled big man.

"So that's it, is it?" Matt crowed, in derision. "The *Lord* wouldn't like it!"

Then, in an instant and totally unexpected change of attitude he leant forward with an elbow on Jackie's desk, and dropped his voice before suggesting a solution to what he saw as a relatively minor problem.

"Sure the Lord doesn't need to know!" he said, in a half whisper.

Jackie laughed.

He had begun reading his New Testament regularly since that happy night on holiday, and knew by now that the God who had effected such a transformation in his life was both all-powerful, and all-knowing. And there was no doubt in his mind, either, that the Divine omniscience would extend even to Sun Bingo cards.

"The Lord would know, and I won't be doing it again, Matt. You may get somebody else," Jackie repeated the message to the despairing man across the table.

All of a sudden Matt rose and stormed out in much the same manner as he had stormed in, mumbling something incoherent about 'fanatical fruitcakes' and inviting Jackie to see him 'again in a week or two when this thing wears off'.

And Matt didn't speak to him again for more than a week!

But others did

The twelve-thirty Bible Study was a revelation. All of the ten or eleven men present shook hands with Jackie individually and told him that they were delighted to hear of his conversion. Then three or four of them, one after another in the prayer time, thanked God for this 'wonderful answer to prayer.'

Following the prayers there came a time when Bibles were handed round and Pete read from John chapter nine about the blind man whom Jesus had healed. He then proceeded to explain the story very simply to the attentive, and obviously interested audience of men in their working wear. Just before the end of the session Pete invited, 'Any Questions?' and some of the men discussed some points that Jackie found hard to understand.

It was wonderful. Jackie felt akin to these men. He had been accepted as one of them from the moment he had entered the room. And he vowed to himself as he walked over to his office afterwards that he would attend that meeting on every possible occasion.

As the week went on, and the news of Sailor Dickey's salvation spread to the outer reaches of the vast shipbuilding complex, men from all over the place, and men he had never met before in his life, turned up in his office. They came from the deepwater dock, the engine sheds, the East Yard, and the fitter's shops, all looking for Jackie Dickey to tell him how thrilled they were to learn that he had come to know the Lord.

Jackie had never even dreamt that there were as many Christians in the whole wide world as this, never mind them all working in Harland & Wolff's!

On Thursday, though, Jackie was somewhat alarmed when one of his mates poked his head in around the door of his office and warned, "You'd better look out, Sailor. There's a man out here in a white hat and he is asking for you!"

The men in the white hats were the big bosses, so Jackie's mind set off in a spin.

What have I done now? he wondered. Am I going to get the sack?

He needn't have worried though.

When 'the man in the white hat' was eventually directed to Jackie's office he entered it with his hand outstretched.

"Hello Jackie, I'm Billy Thompson from the engine sheds," he began, by way of introduction. "And I have just heard some great news. Is it true that you have got saved? I had to come round to meet you and ask you about it myself."

"Yes, it is true," Jackie replied, somewhat surprised that the report of his salvation had made such a big impression on such 'a big shot'. He then proceeded to recount the story once more. The holiday in Majorca, the police cell, the bedroom conversion, and the incredible change were all part of it. But for Billy he could now add the workplace celebration, as well. How excited all the Christians in 'The Yard' had been for the past four days. Apparently some of them had been going back to their local churches where congregations had united in praise to God for this 'miracle of grace', as they called it!

Billy Thompson sat and listened attentively to Jackie's account, interrupting only to mutter a sincere 'Amen' at some particularly powerful points.

When the story was finished, the boss from the engine sheds was obviously touched.

"That's just marvellous, Jackie," he said sincerely, summing it all up. "But before I go I have one thing to say to you, and one question to ask you."

"And what are those things?" Jackie was anxious to know.

"Well what I want to say to you is that I would like you to feel free to call across and see me in the sheds, if you ever want to discuss spiritual matters at any time," Billy Thompson continued in such a caring tone that Jackie was convinced he meant it. "And the question is, have you found a good church to go to yet? It is important that you find yourself a suitable spiritual home. By that I mean a sound evangelical church where you can be happy, and meet plenty of other believers. Fellowship is important."

That was something Jackie had already thought about a time or two, but about which he had not come to any final conclusion. He hadn't been heavily into churches in the past ten or fifteen years, and didn't know much about any of them.

There was one church, however, which had come to his attention over recent months, and he expressed his feelings about it to the big boss turned concerned counsellor.

"I have been giving that some consideration over the last day or two, Billy," he replied, honestly. "My brother in law, Harry, has just got saved about six months ago and he goes to the Assemblies of God on the Comber Road. I was thinking that maybe I could go there with him."

"That would probably be a good idea, Jackie," Billy responded, heartened to discover that the new convert was thinking along such lines.

On the next Sunday, Jackie put his idea into practice. He went with Harry to church.

And Billy had been right, too.

For it turned out to be more than just a good idea.

It was to prove a real spiritual blessing.

Chapter Seventeen

DAD'S BIG DAY OUT

The autumn and winter that followed the summer of salvation were happy seasons for Jackie Dickey. He was constantly amazed at how contented he had become. There was a settled peace in his soul, which he had never believed possible.

During that winter, however, he became aware of a problem that was set to cause him deep concern.

His father was seriously ill.

Anxious not to alarm anyone unduly, and in the old tradition that you just didn't talk about such personal matters, he had tried to keep his ailing condition a secret for as long as possible.

When he did eventually consent to seek medical help he was immediately admitted to the Ulster Hospital, Dundonald, where preliminary investigations soon established that he was suffering from a serious illness. The only possible treatment for his complaint was major surgery, performed as soon as possible.

Jackie just prayed. And prayed. And prayed.

At home, at work, and on the way up to, and back down from his father's home, he prayed for two things. He asked God that He in His power would direct the surgeons when his father returned to the hospital to undergo the vital surgery, and that He would also, in His grace, save his soul.

When he arrived home from work on Tuesday, April 9, 1985, Jackie had a telephone call from his father, the man who had been the subject of most of his recent fervent prayers.

"Jackie, could you get the day off work tomorrow or Thursday?" he asked his son, to whom the request came as rather a bolt from the blue. "I would like you to take me a wee run in your new car. There are some old friends of mine I would like to see again in the County Down."

Now that he wasn't spending every pound he earned on 'the bookies' and booze Jackie had money to spend, so he had passed the driving test and had also bought himself a second-hand blue Vauxhall Cavalier. He was pleased that his father had asked him for 'a wee run' in it, and would be happy to grant him his request, if at all possible.

"Thursday would be better than tomorrow, father," Jackie suggested. " I will ask in work tomorrow to have Thursday off, and I will be pleased to take you wherever you want to go then."

And so it was arranged.

Thursday April 11 was to be Dad's big day out in son's new car. And Mum, for good measure, was coming, too.

When they set out next morning, early, father's first request stop was Portaferry, at the southern tip of the Ards Peninsula, where he made a call in a bar to meet the first of his old acquaintances.

That visit over they crossed on the car ferry to the village of Strangford, on the opposite shore of Strangford Lough, and from there on for a few more miles to Ardglass.

For it was in that fishing village that Alex Dickey wanted to make stop number two.

As they drove into Ardglass, Jackie's father told him his plan.

"You and your mother could go down and have a walk around the village there," he suggested. "I want to call in and see a man in Paddy's Bar."

Having left his father off at the door of the pointed out pub, Jackie and his mother did as they had been enjoined. They had a walk around the village.

Although it was approaching mid-spring it was not a particularly pleasant day, nor was Ardglass a particularly enchanting place. After they had walked down around the harbour, which was more smelly than scenic with the tide out, and looked at the limited range of wares displayed in the limited range of local shops, they found that there was little else left for them to do.

So they returned and sat in the car.

After ten minutes of that, Isobel Dickey was beginning to feel, and look, very cold.

Jackie, becoming acutely conscious of her increasing discomfort, soon figured out a plan to try and do something about it.

"I'll take a walk up into the bar here and see if I my da is nearly finished," he volunteered, and immediately set off.

The bar was almost empty when he entered it. His father was sitting alone at a table in against the wall from where he had been holding a semi-shouted conversation with the proprietor. He had a half-finished bottle of Black Bush whiskey, an almost full bottle of Guinness, and a half-full glass in front of him.

As soon as Jackie swung open the double door, his father saw him and called out, "What are you doing in here, Jackie? You shouldn't be in a place like this."

"Never worry, da," Jackie assured him. "It will be all right. The Lord has taken the desire for the drink away from me."

Alex Dickey then shouted across to the barman, "Bring my son an orange, would you?"

When the ordered orange was brought Jackie began drinking it, but he was the only one drinking anything. Father's glass and bottles remained clustered together, curiously untouched, in the centre of the table.

He said nothing about it though.

Father and son chatted generally.

Then father made a strange statement for a man like him, who had been a lifelong drinker.

"You know, son," he said slowly, thoughtfully. "I don't know what it is, but that drink doesn't taste right. I can't finish it."

Jackie knew the feeling. It had happened to him before.

There was nothing unusual about the drink.

The problem lay with the drinker.

"Praise the Lord!" was his son's instant and inward reaction.

And, "Well then, let's move on somewhere else," was his instant and outward solution. "Mother will be foundered waiting out there in the car."

Alex. Dickey was happy to comply with that proposition, and as they walked back down to the car, Jackie asked, "And where next?"

"Newcastle, if that's O.K." the definitely out for the day dad replied.

Anything would have been O.K. with Jackie. He was both pleased and puzzled all at once by the mystery of the funny tasting drink. Perhaps, he thought, this is the beginning of an answer to my prayers.

In Newcastle the same pattern was applied.

Father made straight for the Donard Bar, and mother and son were expected somehow to amuse themselves, 'up the street'.

Passing the time in Newcastle proved much simpler than passing the time in Ardglass, for there was much more to see in the popular holiday resort. So Jackie and his mother wandered about in carefree fashion for a while, but when they were both becoming hungry, and the chill of the approaching evening began to make itself felt, Isobel Dickey said to her son, "I think you should go and hunt your father out, Jackie. It's about time we were heading for home."

When Jackie made his way into the Donard Bar he found his father alone at a table again. This time though it wasn't Black Bush he had before him. It was three empty Shandy bottles.

"Don't sit down, Jackie. I'm coming," he said, rising, as his son approached him.

As son held the door to allow father to exit, the older man turned to Jackie and remarked, with an air of disbelief, "I can't understand it. I have lost all taste for the whiskey. I just can't touch it any more."

"Praise the Lord!" was Jackie's instant and inward reaction, again.

They drove home from Newcastle, then, and were barely settled into the house when Alex Dickey said to his wife, "Isobel, get on the phone, and phone our Jim. Tell him I want him to come up here at eight o'clock tomorrow morning to take me over to the hospital."

Jim, being the eldest in the family was, in another long held tradition, entrusted with all important decisions and actions in relation to the ageing parents.

Jackie didn't care who took his father to hospital, as long as he had decided to go. He just praised the Lord, instantly, and inwardly, yet again.

On the evening of Monday April 15 the Dickey family were all around their father's bed. The next day was to be the day of his 'big operation', and everyone was feeling tense and nervous. It was one of those situations when everyone wanted to say something significant but nobody could think of anything sufficiently significant to say.

Rev. Moffat had the answer to the almost morbid silence.

"We will pray," he declared softly, and then proceeded to do just that, praying tenderly for Alex in the bed, for the surgery planned for the next morning, for guidance for the medical staff, and for the anxious family.

Jackie, particularly, found the sincerity with which he commended the entire situation to the loving and caring God, whom he had come to know, comforting.

As everyone began to trickle away from the bed Alex Dickey called the minister back. "I would like to speak to you on your own, Rev. Moffat," he requested.

Jackie was thrilled at this, too.

Was father planning to make sure he was right with God? He prayed earnestly all the way down home in the car that he would put his trust in the Lord that evening.

Next day's operation didn't go exactly as planned.

There were complications.

The elderly man suffered a heart seizure on the operating table and the medical team had to fight gallantly to save his life. And after a long struggle they were successful.

His life had been saved, but only just.

Alex Dickey spent the most of a month on a life support machine and on May 15 he passed away.

Jackie believed, though, from a number of observations that he made before he died, that the God who had removed the taste for the drink from him, had replaced it with His new life within him.

And he plans to meet him in heaven.

Chapter Eighteen

THE SAILOR WANTS A WIFE!

The blue Cavalier took Jackie everywhere he needed to go all through the summer of 1985 but as colder autumn and winter days approached it began to rebel at all this driving. It had begun to show its age. And gradually fell apart. Holes appeared in the lower panels, the exhaust dropped off and the battery gave up. Jackie tried in vain to have it valued, but ended up eventually selling it off for a song for the purpose to which it was deemed best suited. Scrap.

Parting with the motor didn't cause Jackie any tremendous heartache for he had never been car crazy anyway, but it did present him with a transport problem. How was he to get from his home off the lower Newtownards Road to church on the Comber Road, Dundonald, every Sunday?

Having prayed for guidance on the matter for some time, Jackie determined to forget about transport, either public or private, and start attending a church near his home. There seemed to be about half a dozen of them within walking distance.

After some consultation with Christian friends Jackie decided that the church where he would feel most at home, and to which he could easily walk, was Newtownards Road Elim Church.

It was early in 1986 when Jackie joined his new Church and for a few Sundays, but only for a few Sundays, he felt awkward and out of place. The fact that this sense of mild embarrassment only lasted a few Sundays was due in part to the warmth of friendship shown to him by most of the members of that Church, but especially by Mrs. Bennett.

On his first Sunday there a little lady in her late sixties, with white hair, bright eyes and a big black handbag, made her away across to him as he was sidling slowly out of the service, wondering who he could speak to.

"Good morning, son," she greeted the newcomer cheerily. "Glad to have you with us. And what's your name?"

"I'm Jackie Dickey," came Jackie's reply. "I live round in Frome Street."

"Well I'm Sarah Bennett," the little lady volunteered, and then set about giving Jackie her own personal history, the history of her family for the past two generations, the history of the church from the middle of the twentieth century, concluding, out on the footpath, with an enthusiastic appraisal of their current pastor. 'This man we have now' as she called him.

As he walked home afterwards Jackie felt that he now knew more about the church than many of the others who had been in it for years, but he liked Mrs. Bennett. He may even have to take her up sometime on her parting offer of the morning, which was, "If you feel you ever need any help about anything in the church, Jackie, just ask me."

Jackie loved the Lord, and he loved the whole-hearted worship of the Lord in Newtownards Road Elim Church, and with the arrival of spring he had begun to feel as though he belonged there. He had become an integral part of the fellowship.

He had, however, another pastime that occupied most of his non-praying, non-praising, non-listening time. It was the pursuit which saw him amongst the first to arrive at the church, and amongst the last to leave it at every service, keeping his eyes and ears, but particularly his eyes, open all the time.

And it was the purpose of this pursuit that he was forced to admit one Saturday night after the Youth Fellowship. Although he could hardly have been described as 'a youth' at touching thirty years of age, Jackie liked the Youth Fellowship. It was a lot different from the Welder's Club, where he had once spent his Saturdays, but it was where he now wanted to go, and you would just never know…

The speakers that night had been missionaries from the Congo in central Africa. They seemed frustrated that they were unable to carry on with the work as they once had done, because of declining health, but they talked a lot about 'open doors' and 'fields white already to harvest'.

At the end of the service the missionary couple offered an invitation to anyone interested to stay behind and speak to either of them 'about the mission field, during the tea'.

In keeping with his eyes open, ears open, stay as long as you can, see as much as you can, policy Jackie stayed behind. It wasn't that he was particularly interested in going to the Congo above anywhere else.

He would go to the Congo if he had to, but he would just have been as happy to go to either Cork or Coleraine, if it would achieve his aim. He did love the Lord and he also appreciated the life of dedicated service which the couple whom he had just heard had spent in Africa. But white fields and mud huts were not uppermost in his mind at that moment.

The missionary lady must have mistaken his intention in remaining behind, though. For she balanced her tea and biscuits across and sat down beside him. Perhaps this obviously unattached young man would be a candidate for a Christian mission in the Congo.

As they chatted together the lady told Jackie about the privileges and challenges of what she described as 'full-time service for the Lord'.

When they had spoken for almost ten minutes and the ardent missionary advocate realized that her whole-hearted encouragement had only evoked at best a half-hearted response, she enquired, in gentle exasperation, "Tell me the truth, Jackie. What do you want in life?"

"Well to tell you the truth I want a wife!" came the honest reply.

The missionary lady smiled, bit into her last biscuit which had become soggy since being soaked in split tea, and gave up. If that was all the man wanted he surely didn't need to go to Africa to find it!

The quest proved more difficult than it would have at first appeared, for the wife-hunting Sailor had created in his mind a list of desirable qualities that this, for so far fantasy, woman would possess.

She would have to be young, attractive, unattached and Christian.

And most of the women whom he had met up until that point hadn't passed on one or more of his preconditions. For they were either too old for him, unattractive to him, committed to somebody else, or unsaved.

Jackie had begun to panic. But surely an all-loving, all-powerful God could sort something out for him in a city the size of Belfast!

In late May, Jackie saw a glimmer of light on the horizon. It had suddenly begun to twinkle over the still-shut gate into the garden of love.

This hint of hope came in the form of a Sunday morning announcement by Pastor Napier, and concerned a planned combined Pentecostal crusade in The Ulster Hall, in the city centre, during the coming September. And they urgently needed volunteers to form a huge combined choir from all the churches, to lead the praise.

This, thought Jackie, is my big chance.

A combined choir from all the churches! Surely there would be somebody there to meet all his requirements!

On the way out of church he talked to Mrs. Bennett about it.

"You see that choir they are talking about, Mrs. Bennett," he began. "I know I'm not a brilliant singer, but do you think they would have the likes of me in it?"

"Of course they would, Jackie," Mrs. Bennett replied, enthusiastically. She was one of these wee women who was so positive about everything. "And what's more," she went on to whisper, leaning over towards Jackie and planting her elbow firmly in his side, "You might even find yourself a nice young girl over there."

"That would be good, Mrs. Bennett," Jackie said, smiling benevolently, not having the heart to say what he really meant, which was, "What do you think I am going for, woman dear?"

So spurred on by his own ambitions and that boost from Mrs. Bennett, Jackie signed 'the paper in the porch', volunteering his singing services, such as they were, to the combined choir.

The 'over there' of his spiritual mentor's hopeful forecast, was Beersbridge Road Elim Church, where the first practice for the new choir was to be held on the first Friday evening in June at eight o'clock.

True to his established pattern Jackie arrived well before the starting time to survey the incoming talent. And he waited and waited and waited. But not a lot of talent turned up.

About five to eight an elderly lady with a list stuck into the back of a music book came over to him, "Are you Jackie Dickey?" she wanted to know. She had probably been able to figure who he was for there were only three men in the room as far as Jackie could see, and she had already been to the other two!

"Yes, I am," the new recruit replied, going on to ask, "Is this all that's coming?"

"No, I think there should be one or two more yet," she said, moving on to check someone else off her list.

When the 'one or two more' did eventually arrive the lady in charge of operations began to explain about the choir, the importance and purpose of the crusade, and the pieces that she proposed they should practice.

While she was talking away earnestly, Jackie was looking around eagerly, and when he had finished his hasty review he just whispered a panic prayer to himself.

"Oh, Lord have mercy on me," he breathed in desperation.

There wasn't a female under forty in the whole place!

Every Friday night in June and on into July, Jackie attended the choir practices. And it seemed that from the second night onwards the choir-mistress would announce at the end of the session, "And we have some good news. There will be four, or five, or seven more people coming to the practice next week."

So Jackie kept his heart up for another week. Maybe next week would be *his* week.

And when next week came all the new people who turned up to join the practice were even older than those of the previous week!

Friday July 4 was to be their last practice before a two-week break for 'the Twelfth fortnight' holiday. And Friday July 4 had been no more promising on the 'I want a wife' front for Jackie than any other night had been. There had been five new additions that evening, five fine singers all in their fifties, a man, a spinster, two mothers and a grandmother.

It was a fine, warm summer evening as Jackie walked home to Frome Street. The sound of practising bands and the deafening rhythm of Lambeg drums echoed all over East Belfast.

Jackie kicked a Coke can left by a litterlout and sent it spinning away down the pavement ahead of him. As he watched it topple off the kerb and stop at the wheel of a parked car, Jackie spoke aloud to his heavenly Father about his very earthly problem.

"Lord I know Your ways are not my ways," he began, seriously, "but is there nothing You can do about this situation? I have been going to this choir thing now for five weeks and I am looking for a genuine Christian girl about my own age. And Lord, You in your wisdom must know that things are going from bad to worse. Is there no way Lord, that You could just adapt things somehow? I mean with all the Christian girls in this city there must be something You could do. In Jesus' name I ask it. Amen."

With that he left it with the Lord. And a week later he went off for a holiday to Jack and Mina's cottage outside Ballyhalbert on the Ards Peninsula.

It was when sitting in the sun outside that cottage one day that the Lord revealed His plan for Jackie, to Jackie, by another verse of Scripture, which flashed into his mind. And it afforded him a different aspect on 'this choir thing'.

It was a verse he had heard in a church somewhere, but he couldn't remember where, and it came with a striking force to him. The words burned into his brain.

'Whether you eat or drink, or whatever you do, do all to the glory of God,' was their message.

'Whatever you do, do all to the glory of God'.

Jackie was convicted. Caught. Challenged.

He had joined the choir to meet the members, spot the talent, and get himself a girlfriend. And the glory of God certainly hadn't played a big part in his planning!

It was strange. It was as though a voice spoke to him and said, "You were right, Jackie. My ways are not your ways. But go back to the choir, enjoy it, sing for My glory, and leave your future in My hands."

And when the choir practices resumed towards the end of the month, Jackie did that. He went back, and instead of keeping his eye on the door, expecting his big surprise to enter at any moment and sweep at him off his feet he kept his eye on the conductor, and sang heartily to the glory of God.

His big surprise was that he actually enjoyed it!

The combined crusade in the Ulster Hall began on Sunday September 21 with big crowds attending from the very first night. And as the week progressed more people came.

Jackie loved it. Standing up with the choir at the front of a packed hall singing the praises of God, gave him a special thrill.

An even greater thrill was in store for him on the Thursday night, though.

At the end of every crusade meeting audiotapes of the service were on sale in the lobby of the Ulster Hall. Jackie never usually bought any of these, but he liked to remain around, chatting to people he knew. It would be almost twenty-four hours to the next meeting, and he didn't like that.

On Thursday night he was standing near the tape-selling table when he saw a young woman whom he knew approaching it. They had spoken a number of times before, but only casually.

That night, however, the young woman called Mandy, whom Jackie understood to have been recently widowed, came across to where he was standing and asked with a smile, "Are you not buying yourself a tape of the service?"

"No I'm not," Jackie replied, adding by way of explanation, "I haven't enough money with me."

That was true. Jackie couldn't afford to buy a tape every night, so he hadn't enough money with him. But that was only part of the story. The real reason why he didn't want a tape was that he didn't have a tape-recorder to play it on!

There was something, though, about the spontaneous warmth of this Mandy's approach that appealed to him straight away.

"Never worry then, I'll buy one for you!" she volunteered.

With that Mandy opened a purse she was carrying and produced a roll of crisp and crinkly ten-pound notes. Jackie's eyes nearly popped out of his head!

As Mandy crossed over to join the haphazard crowd at the table, still clutching her roll of notes, the thirty-year old wife-seeker's legs had gone weak and his mind had set off in a whirl.

Here was not only a young and attractive widow, but she was also a young and attractive *Christian* widow.

And not only a young and attractive Christian widow but also a *rich* and young and attractive Christian widow.

Jackie talked to God again, there and then. He was not coming in desperation this time, but in delight.

"Thank You, Lord," he said. "She'll do. I would settle for that one."

And just before Mandy returned to press a tape, which he had no means of hearing, into his hand, there remained only one more matter which he had to clear up with his Heavenly Guide.

"And by the way Lord," he went on humbly. "Thank You for teaching me that Your ways are not my ways. And help me now to talk to Mandy, for she looks as though she was worth waiting for!"

Chapter Nineteen

WHERE ARE YOU, GOD?

God answered Jackie's prayer.

He helped Sailor the wife-seeker to talk to Mandy and to invite her out for a meal after the September crusade.

Beginning at that meal in Holywood, and then when they met again almost a month later, Jackie heard some aspects of the history of Mandy that he didn't already know.

He had been familiar with the bare bones of the story. Mandy was a young widow, and that was nearly all he knew about her. So she, as their 'dates' began to increase in frequency, filled him in on the finer details.

They went something like this…

Mandy Hutchinson was born and reared in East Belfast. On leaving school she went to work packing bread in the Sunblest Bakery on the Castlereagh Road.

Her older brother Paul loved motorbikes and had a friend called Thomas Williams who was also 'bike mad'. This shared passion led to Thomas becoming a frequent visitor to the Hutchinson home.

Thomas hadn't made many visits, however, until he discovered that Paul had more than just an interest in 'bikes'. He also had a rather attractive sister.

It wasn't long, either, until he had asked Mandy if she would like to 'come for a spin on the pillion'.

Mandy, the fun-loving teenager, was always game for a bit of an adventure, so she was only too happy to accept his invitation. It was a totally new, and very exhilarating experience. The roar and smell of the bike, the wind streaming through her hair, and her arms locked around the bent forward body in front, all served to give her a bit of a buzz.

Thomas became an even more frequent caller at Paul's house after that. The aims of his visits had changed, though. Now he wasn't calling to show his friend the latest accessory he had acquired for his bike, but to take his sister out on it!

This early casual, carefree acquaintance gradually developed into a more permanent relationship and Thomas and Mandy were married in November 1983.

The newly married couple moved to the County Down town of Newtownards, to live but in May 1985 an ominous black cloud appeared on the horizon of their lives.

Thomas took ill and was admitted to the Royal Victoria Hospital in Belfast where a series of tests confirmed the initial suspicions of the medical staff. He was suffering from leukaemia.

Two things happened during those tense days of illness and hospital visitation.

The first was that one day at her husband's bedside Mandy met a chap called Jackie Dickey who had come up to visit Thomas, for they both worked together in the ship repair yard in Harland and Wolff's. This was nothing more than a passing introduction and neither of them thought anything more of it at the time. They were both, to obviously different degrees, concerned for the health and welfare of the man in the bed.

The other important thing, which occurred in those trying times, was that Thomas, who was very ill, and who had once been a committed Christian but had latterly lost the joy of his salvation, was restored to the Lord.

A number of times when he had a temporary respite from his intensive treatment, and was well enough to be at home, Thomas had asked Mandy, who had seldom ever attended church in her life, to accompany him to a Sunday service.

The young wife always made some excuse.

She didn't feel well, she said.

She had the dinner to prepare, she said.

Churches gave her 'the creeps', she said.

Thomas was disappointed, but Mandy was adamant.

She would not be going to any church.

On the Sunday mornings when Thomas attended church, Mandy was left to vent her anger and frustration at God and her circumstances on the vegetables at home.

'God, if you exist,' she would growl out her grudging grievance, as she peeled the potatoes, 'don't let Thomas die. If You are as great and powerful and loving as he seems to think You are, You will do something for him, and soon.'

Those prayers weren't answered, however.

Thomas passed away into the presence of the Lord in January 1986.

Mandy was devastated.

During the traumatic days of the funeral and immediately afterwards she found that the only way in which she could even appear to cope was to keep herself constantly doped on nerve tablets. Otherwise she would have been out of her mind.

In the cold and lonely winter days that followed Mandy lived with Thomas' parents who were extremely kind to her. Her in-laws were sincere Christian people who attended their church every Sunday but as she had done with their son, so she did with them. She declined all invitations to accompany them to their place of worship.

The onset of spring with slightly warmer and slightly longer days and bursting buds in the city parks did little to relieve the gloom that had settled on Mandy's mind. As she tried to wean herself off the drugs she had been taking, she lapsed into an attitude of unremitting resentment.

What was the point in all these people going to church and praying? she wondered. Had she not prayed desperately for God to spare the life of her husband, and He hadn't heard her? At least if He had heard her, He just hadn't bothered to answer.

All this emphasis on 'religion' as she called it, and going out to church meant that Sundays were usually her worst, and most bitter days.

During the week her work brought some relief to the loneliness and misery, but on Sundays when Thomas' heartbroken parents sought their solace in God and amongst their fellow Christians, Mandy felt particularly embittered.

On one such morning, when left alone in the house, she went into her bedroom to 'make the bed' and tidy the room. She was feeling absolutely empty, fiercely angry, and completely cheated.

The fact that most of her relations assured her that Thomas was 'in heaven', meant nothing to her. All that mattered to her was that regardless of where he was, there remained one place that he wasn't, and that was with her.

Straightening herself up from folding in the bedcovers she crossed to the wardrobe and banged on it furiously with her fist.

"Where are you, God?" she yelled, in an agonized amalgam of deep despair and downright defiance. "You don't exist. I know You don't exist! Or if You do exist You just don't care!"

Then Mandy slumped back on to the bed, exhausted from that violent expression of her usually repressed emotions.

"You let my Thomas die, when I begged You to let him live," she sobbed, through her hands.

"And now what is going to happen to me?"

Chapter Twenty

I KNOW HOW YOU FEEL

For months the agony continued.

Emptiness and nothingness bred resentment and rebellion.

In May 1986, Thomas' mother suggested a holiday with a difference to her distraught daughter-in-law. This would be, what she considered, 'the kind of break Mandy needed.'

Mrs. Williams arranged for the young widow to go and spend a couple of weeks with some Christian friends she knew in Newcastle-upon-Tyne. Her idea in sending Mandy there to stay was that the young mother in that home, Rhoda, had passed through the horrible trauma of losing a partner. Her first husband had been killed, some years before, in the Troubles in Northern Ireland.

Rhoda had by then remarried, and she and her second husband, Steve, had two lovely children and a happy home.

Mandy's holiday in that home proved to be a turning point in her life, both emotionally and spiritually.

When Steve was out at work and the children were otherwise occupied, Rhoda and Mandy had many heart-to-heart conversations. She found it strange at first, but Mandy found herself locked in to listen to this capable and confident young woman. There was something compelling about both her conversation and her character.

There were at least two ways in which Rhoda differed from all the others who had attempted to sympathise with her before.

She hadn't been speaking to her long until she realized that this person spoke from a background of painful experience. Rhoda didn't say, as so many sincere and well-meaning people had done, "Oh that must have been awful for you!" She was able to sit across the table from Mandy and say, with a tear in her eye, "I know how you feel, Mandy. I've been there."

And that made such a difference.

The second way in which Mandy noticed that her hostess was different from those she had previously encountered, was in attitude. Rhoda was a Christian and spoke readily and easily about her faith. She wasn't blaming God for what had happened to her. Nor was she feeling sorry for herself.

Instead, Rhoda was relying upon God for strength and guidance in her life. And she was also praising God for leading her to her new husband, Steve, and for affording her the privilege of starting a family.

Although Mandy still felt bitter and cheated at the death of Thomas, yet she found that she had no answer to Rhoda's calm confidence in her acceptance of her circumstances. And when the opportunity arose Rhoda told Mandy of her need.

Thomas was a Christian, and was now in heaven, and if Mandy ever wanted to see him again she would have to be saved, she told her.

This was all news to Mandy. She had never been one for going to church much, and had never encountered any genuine Christians until she had met Thomas and his parents. There had been one or two she had come across in her work that had claimed to be 'saved' but she had just dismissed them as 'good-living kill-joys'.

On her first Sunday in Newcastle Mandy accompanied Steve and Rhoda to their church where she heard again what Rhoda had already told her. If she ever intended to be in heaven, she 'must be born again'.

The message of the Gospel so graciously presented by her hostess began to make an impression on Mandy, for it came with such utter conviction and with such tender care. It was obvious that Steve and his wife were happy in their faith and confident about their future.

After she had been there for just a few days Mandy began to lie awake for hours at night. She found it almost impossible to rid her mind of these matters.

If I had died, and not Thomas, she reasoned, then I would not be in heaven, for I am not saved. And if I ever want to be in heaven, and if I ever expect to see him again, then I will need to be saved.

Mandy was still mixed up and miserable. And the tablets, to which she still occasionally returned in times of acute distress, afforded no relief. Her problem now was not self-pity and a passion to shout at God, but rather a craving for satisfaction and a desire to seek God.

It was almost midnight on the night of Tuesday 3rd June 1986, when Mandy slid out of bed and onto her knees at her bedside. She had never prayed much to God before, other than a series of selfish and strident demands during Thomas' illness, which had been more like commands than prayers. Now, though, she was coming, a humble, broken woman to crave forgiveness, and seek salvation.

"Lord, I am a sinner, and I want You to forgive me," she said slowly and softly, struggling for the right words. "I know that Jesus died for me and I want to come to Him. Please make me Your child and take me to Your heaven."

She paused for a minute, and then went on.

"And Lord I want to thank You for bringing me to meet Steve and Rhoda. Please help me to live for You the way they do."

There was a second pause. This time though, she found that she had no more to say so she whispered a reverent 'Amen" which she gathered was the proper thing to do, and clambered back into the bed.

Now things were different.

A sense of peace and quiet satisfaction flowed over her being, covering it gently, smoothing away all the anger and unrest. It was just like when she used to watch the stretching out width of the shallow shafts of the incoming tide levelling away all the roughness from the churned up sand on the beach at Ballyholme, near Bangor, back in Northern Ireland.

In less than an hour she had drifted off into a sound and settled sleep.

Next morning at breakfast she told Rhoda what had happened. "I trusted the Lord in my bedroom last night, Rhoda," she said simply.

"Oh Mandy that's wonderful!" her hostess made no attempt to conceal her elation. "Praise the Lord! That's a wonderful answer to prayer!" she exclaimed

Later that evening Steve and Rhoda arrived home with a present for their guest. Mandy had been surprised all day at how happy it was possible to feel, as a Christian, and she was even more surprised when she unwrapped the small package Rhoda gave her.

Her eyes danced with absolute delight when she discovered that it contained her first ever, and very own Bible.

During the remaining days of her stay in Newcastle, Steve and Rhoda outlined some basic guidelines for Christian living to the new convert, and they could do so with confidence for they lived their own lives to the standards they were advocating.

It was important to read the Bible every day, they said.

It was important to talk to God in prayer every day, they told her.

And they also recommended that when she arrived home, Mandy should begin attending a lively evangelical church, and make herself some Christian friends.

After a strangely tearful, yet joyful, parting with her new friends, and also her fellow-Christians, in Newcastle, Mandy returned to Belfast, and sought to act on their counsel.

One of Thomas' sisters, Lynn, attended Beersbridge Road Elim Church in the city, and Mandy began going along there with her. The story of Mandy's conversion had reached Belfast before she had been able to return in person, and so she was immediately and warmly welcomed in that church, and felt at home amongst the members, many of whom she already knew.

And it was in a Sunday morning service there that she had heard the September Crusade in the Ulster Hall announced.

The prospect of more than a week of praise, prayer and preaching sounded exciting to the new believer who was so happy in her newly found faith.

She determined that she wouldn't miss a night, and didn't.

It was on the Thursday night of the first week, too, that she met Jackie Dickey again.

And bought him a tape.

Chapter Twenty-One

ALL I WANT FOR CHRISTMAS

In late October and throughout November, Jackie and Mandy began to see each other more frequently. They were happy together, and each one, unknown to the other, had begun to make plans for the future.

Jackie knew that Mandy was an answer to his many impassioned prayers. God had, he firmly believed, led them together. He would love to be in a position to ask Mandy to marry him, but there was one matter which had begun to cause him some concern at that time, and which seemed to shatter any prospects of wedded bliss.

It was the thought of possible redundancy.

In the autumn of 1986 it was announced that there were to be massive pay-offs in the shipyard. Some sources were even predicting that the ship repair yard, where Jackie worked, was to close completely.

How then, he wondered could he go to this lovely Christian young woman and say to her, "I love you, Mandy. I want to marry you, Mandy. But I have no job, Mandy. And no money, Mandy"?

Mandy's plan for the future was different.

She knew that there was a possibility that Jackie could lose his job. They had talked about that more than once.

She knew also that Jackie had health problems, which had come as a direct result of his earlier alcohol addiction.

Neither of these considerations rated very highly with her, however. They were, in her opinion quite serious, but by no means insurmountable.

She loved Jackie, just in the same way as he loved her, and yearned for the security of a stable relationship, the happiness of a shared home, and the love and laughter of children.

During November the young couple had established the pattern of attending the Sunday morning service in Newtownards Road Elim Church together, and then walking round to Jackie's aunt Mina and uncle Jack for dinner.

The couple, who had been like a second set of parents to Jackie, were very fond of this pleasant woman he had started to bring around the place. She was lively and attractive yet at the same time both down-to-earth and friendly. From her very first visit there Mandy had just fitted in like one of the family.

On the first Sunday in December, Mandy and Mina were washing up the dinner dishes in the tiny kitchen, leaving Jackie to discuss matters of such grave and local importance as the forthcoming possible redundancies in, and bleak looking future for, 'The Yard', with his uncle in the living room.

Almost up to her elbows in soapsuds, Mandy who was washing, to allow Mina, who knew every square inch of the kitchen, to 'dry and put away', turned to Jackie's aunt and asked with a smile, but almost stunning suddenness, "Do you know what I want for Christmas, Mina?"

"No, I don't Mandy. What would you like for Christmas, dear?" the older woman's curiosity was aroused at this out of the blue somewhat curious question.

"I would like a ring," Mandy told her.

"Oh you mean you would like me to buy you a nice wee dress ring, dear," Mina went on, presuming to read Mandy's mind but secretly rather surprised by her quite uncharacteristic forwardness.

"No Mina, I don't mean you to buy me a nice wee dress ring," Mandy explained, with a coy smile and her voice dropped to a confidential whisper. "I mean Jackie to buy me a nice wee engagement ring."

All drying operations were immediately subjected to a short suspension.

Mina held a half-dried dinner plate in her left hand and a half-wet drying cloth drooped from her right.

"I'm sure that would be lovely," she responded at length, with the warmth of one welcoming a woman-to-woman shared aspiration. She would most certainly be happy with the prospect of Mandy as a partner for the man who was practically her son.

Then another thought struck her.

"Just as a matter of interest, have you told Jackie about this?" she enquired, beaming broadly.

"No I haven't, Mina," Mandy had to confess, with a mischievous twinkle in her eye. "But I promise you I will. And soon!"

Having given such an undertaking to Jackie's caring aunt, Mandy knew she had to act upon it, and did, that evening.

As Jackie and she were sitting outside her home in Newtownards in his silver Datsun, before parting, Mandy brought up the same subject, in the same manner, as she had done with Mina. Only this time it was to a different person, and with a more direct purpose!

"I hope you don't mind me asking this, Jackie," she began, pretending to be ever so bashful, "But do you know what I would like for Christmas?"

"No, I don't, love. What would you like for Christmas?" Jackie was pleased to be able to ask that question for he had been wondering what a maybe soon to be redundant shipyard worker like him, could buy a rich, as he imagined it, young widow like Mandy, to mark their first Christmas together. He would have to make it a good one whatever it was, and if she could tell him something that she would like, that would just be great! He would spend every penny he possessed to buy it for her, if possible.

Mandy didn't waste much time in making her request, when given the chance.

"I would like a ring," she said with a short, loving laugh.

"You mean a nice wee dress ring?" Jackie's initial reaction was exactly the same as his aunt Mina's had been.

She could hardly believe it! Mandy shook her head in mock disbelief, and just laughed out loud. Did these folk from Frome Street not know that there were other kinds of rings in the world as well as dress rings?

"No Jackie. I don't mean a nice wee dress ring," she replied, and then leaning over she put her arm around his shoulder and whispered into his ear, "To tell you the truth I mean a nice wee engagement ring!"

The colour drained from Jackie's face.

The power disappeared from his arms and legs and they began to shake uncontrollably.

Speech had gone.

Jackie Dickey was in shock.

He had wanted to marry Mandy, but had been afraid to ask her, because of problems with his health and possible unemployment. She, however, wanted to marry him and seemed to have no such hang-ups.

The power to produce sound returned to his voice box before the power to produce sense returned to his brain.

His first garbled attempts to respond sounded like a toddler's first attempts to ask his first question. "I mean...what about?...how would we?...if I have no job...it takes money, I mean, it takes money...how could ...?"

Mandy stopped him and assured him that all would be well.

They loved each other, and the God who had loved them, had saved them both in difficult situations, and had by His grace and wisdom brought them together, could look after them for the rest of their lives, if they committed their marriage into His bountiful hands.

That eventually began to make sense to Jackie. He had been guilty before of trying to organize his own life after having given God a few instructions as to how he felt it should be done. It had only been when he had rolled the matter unreservedly into the hands of his Heavenly Guide that He had taken control and worked it all out.

Mandy loved Jackie, and no argument about possible earthly obstacles could shake her faith in Divine provision.

And Mandy got her ring!

On Christmas morning, after the service in Newtownards Road Elim Church Jackie and Mandy announced their engagement, and Mandy proudly showed everyone her fist Christmas present from Jackie, her ring.

Both of them were very happy, and began to plan for a wedding in the spring of the following year.

Their plans seemed to take a knock, however, when it was announced officially, in January 1987, that the ship repair yard in Harland and Wolff's was to close, and all the staff employed there were to be declared redundant.

Although a singular blow to their future security, Jackie's redundancy proved to be, in a strange sense, a double blessing. For it had the effect of forcing both he and Mandy to commit the planning of their lives together all the more fervently to the Lord, relying upon Him alone for direction, and it also brought with it a timely financial bonus.

Jackie and Mandy were married in Newtownards Road Elim Church on Saturday 11th April, 1987.

And Jackie's redundancy payment helped them meet the wedding expenses, and procure some essentials for setting up home together.

They now belonged to each other.

And were depending, for everything, upon God.

Chapter Twenty-Two

MAKE YOUR MIND UP TIME

In the early hours of Sunday 9th August, Mandy shook her husband awake.

"Hurry up, Jackie. Get up!" she ordered him urgently. "I have terrible pain. There is something badly wrong. I think I am going into labour."

Jackie jumped to the sudden call.

He was on the floor and struggling into his clothes before he had really recovered his senses. Mandy and he were expecting their first child. He knew that. He had, however been given to understand that it would be some time yet before it arrived.

This was a rather rude awakening.

When they arrived, in haste, at the Ulster Hospital, Mandy was admitted immediately to the Maternity Unit and Jackie was left to sit in a waiting area, trying to come to grips with what exactly it was that was going on. He could have returned home, but he had no desire to return home. It would be better to be on hand, he thought, to be available if anyone needed to contact him for any reason.

Just before eight o'clock a doctor appeared in the waiting area where Jackie had spent the previous two and more hours sitting down for five minutes and pacing around for ten. His countenance was grave.

"I came out to tell you Mr. Dickey that we are concerned both for your wife's condition and for the survival of the baby. Both of them are in danger. There may come a time when we will have to ask you who it is you would prefer us to concentrate on saving, either your wife or the baby. You may be asked to sign a form indicating your choice."

Jackie was thunderstruck.

That was his second, and by far the more stunning, shock of the morning.

Having been pummelled into consciousness was something he could easily cope with in the circumstances, but to make that kind of a stark, final decision would be beyond him.

"I'm sorry doctor," he replied, filling up with tears. "I don't think I could make that choice. I couldn't choose which of the two I wanted to live, because if I did that I would be choosing which of them I wanted to die. And that would be same as signing their death warrant."

"O.K. Mr. Dickey," the doctor conceded. "We will leave it meantime, and we will do what we can. But think about it, for you may yet be asked to make up your mind."

"You do the best you can, as you say. I will think about it and pray about it," Jackie replied, and the doctor returned to his work.

In just over half-an-hour he was back.

Jackie had lost all sense of time or place or even existence.

He had spent the interval in a state of confused panic. He didn't seem to be able to think straight, and he couldn't pray properly. All he could do was bow his head, down somewhere between his knees and the floor, and cry out in agony, "Oh God, please help. Please help us!"

"The news is partly good and partly not so good," was the medical man's message. "The baby has been safely delivered. It is a boy, but he is very much premature. He is only two and a half pounds weight, and if he survives he may have difficulties. We have rushed him down to our premature unit for specialist attention. As for your wife, she is still gravely ill. Neither of them is by any means out of the woods yet."

When the ward staff considered it appropriate Jackie was allowed in to see Mandy very briefly. She looked awful, pale and washed out, and surrounded by a frightening assortment of medical hardware.

It was obvious to the perplexed husband that his wife was heavily sedated.

When she opened her eyes Jackie whispered down to her, "It's a boy."

An attempt at a smile pulled at the corners of Mandy's dry mouth. "Yes, I know," she croaked back feebly. "We will call him Jonathan."

"That's right, love. We will call him Jonathan," Jackie assured her in hushed tones, but he was unsure whether she had heard him or not. Mandy had lapsed back into unconsciousness, battling for life.

Months before, when neither of them could have even have had any notion of the trauma that had now befallen them, Jackie and Mandy had decided that if it was a boy, he should be called Jonathan. They had both loved the Bible story of Jonathan's loyal love for David, and decided that their little boy, if they had a little boy, would have both names. He would be named Jonathan David, but be known as Jonathan.

On leaving Mandy's bedside Jackie was still a very worried husband and now, father. The joy of the birth of their firstborn had been eclipsed by the illness of both mother and child.

When he returned to the waiting area he began to call upon God. He had already prayed in desperation, but although Jonathan and Mandy were both still clinging to life, there was still much to pray for.

It seemed to him that the heavens were as brass. Nothing dramatic or miraculous was happening when he had believed that it would.

"Where are You, God?" he ended up praying.

"Oh God, if You can hear me, please spare Mandy and the baby," was his plaintive plea.

Then the thought struck him that he didn't need to pray alone. It was Sunday morning, and still before morning service time.

Finding a pay phone he rang Pastor Napier from Newtownards Road Elim Church and poured out his heart to him, letting him know of all the problems. Jackie told his pastor of Mandy's critical condition, of their premature baby Jonathan, who was just about the size and weight of a bag of sugar, and of the doctors' concerns for his survival.

The pastor was touched by the plight of the young couple and their desperately ill little premature baby.

"Lay hold upon God, Jackie," was his advice to the almost frantic father.

"We will be praying especially for you all at the services today," was his promise.

While Jackie tried to calm his troubled mind by doing as he had been counselled, 'laying hold upon God', Pastor Napier proved as good as his word. He abandoned his address at the morning service and after he had outlined the desperate dilemma of the Dickeys, the church members embarked on an impassioned prayer session for Mandy and Jonathan, that God would by His grace, and in His mercy, spare both of them to Jackie.

And Mrs. Bennett commenced a period of prayer and fasting.

The evening service that Sunday took exactly the same form as the morning service had done. It was a period of intense prayer to God for Jackie, Mandy and Jonathan.

And Mrs. Bennett continued her period of prayer and fasting.

Those prayers were heard, and answered, too.

God heard the pleading of His people and directed the skill of the doctors and nurses in that maternity unit. During the day Mandy's condition stabilized and Jonathan survived, but just about. It was still 'touch and go' with him for days.

Many fervent prayers were offered over the next day or two, not only by the members of their own church, but in church fellowships all over Belfast. And by Monday evening a miracle had occurred.

Mandy, whose life had at one time been in very real danger, was able to walk, with Jackie's help, down to the premature baby unit, where the new parents stood in awe, gazing in wonder at their tiny little son.

He was in a special incubator, surrounded by wires and tubes, but he was alive. He had made it so far.

Jackie and Mandy were still not able to hold or handle the miniature miracle of life, but they could at least see him. And that was a start.

As they turned away from the incubator, for Jackie to assist his weak wife in her soft-shoe shuffle back to the ward, the now happier husband squeezed Mandy's hand, and offered his heartfelt gratitude to God.

His expression of warm appreciation turned out to be just as simple, but every bit as sincere, as his panic prayers of the day before had been.

Big tears rolled unchecked down his cheeks as he said, hoarsely, "Thank You, God. Thank You."

Chapter Twenty-Three

JUST TRUST ME

Mandy grew stronger every day and within a week was well enough to be discharged from hospital. That in itself was an answer to prayer and a tribute to medical skill. But baby Jonathan was a different matter. His condition was still giving the doctors cause for deep concern.

In those critical early days of his life the tiny infant stopped breathing a number of times. And on each occasion he was successfully resuscitated.

When the anxious parents made their daily visit to the hospital to see their little son, the situation always seemed to be something the same.

"Oh we thought we had lost him today, but he is O.K. now," a nurse would possibly report.

Or, "He doesn't seem to be making a lot of progress," a doctor would remark. "It is only the ventilator that is keeping him alive."

After a few weeks of this constant uncertainty, this watching but not touching their seriously ill baby son, this daily dwelling in deep depression, Mandy cried out to her equally distressed but not quite so demonstrative husband, in despair, "Jackie I can't take this any more. This can't go on. This endless waiting of death, this expecting to be told some day that Jonathan has died, is getting to me. I'm sorry but I just can't cope with it any longer."

She had hit rock bottom in the slough of despond.

Jackie tried to console her by telling her that God was in control, that His will would be done, and that Christian people in many parts were praying for Jonathan at that very minute, no matter what very minute it was.

Mandy heard all that he said, and she knew that all he said was so true.

But it all sounded so trite as well.

She had heard it all before.

It was quite easy to say that 'God's will would be done', or that 'All things work together for good to those who love God,' when you weren't involved.

When it was *her baby* that was possibly about to die, though, Mandy found it more difficult to be so spiritual, so philosophical, or so patient.

The perpetual pressure was eating into her.

Why, she wondered privately, could God not just heal her little boy now, this minute, perform a mighty miracle or even something less spectacular but equally effective, and set her free from this unremitting emotional misery?

The answer to all her inner questions came one Sunday morning in September.

The young couple had gone out to the morning service in Newtownards Road Elim Church, as usual. On the way in many genuinely interested and deeply caring prayer partners had been asking about 'the wee baby'.

The response to such earnest enquiries was invariably, "Oh he's very much the same. Still in the incubator and on the ventilator, and by no means out of danger yet. Please keep praying."

It was hard for them, especially Mandy, the mother.

She just kept wondering, "How long is this going to go on for? How long can God let this agony last?"

The worship began with a period of animated chorus singing. There was much joy and rejoicing in that wholehearted expression of praise to God.

As they sat there, with the crowd singing enthusiastically around them,

'Jesus is alive,

Jesus is alive,

His is the grace that sets me free'... Mandy was one of the few who hadn't been singing. She had been sitting, silently transfixed, staring into space, seeing nothing.

Slowly, gradually, she became aware that something unusual was happening to her.

The sound of the singing, which was continuing, as exuberant as ever, seemed to melt away into a mellow distance, from where it provided a beautiful melodious background in her mind. Then she felt that she had somehow become detached from her surroundings, that she was no longer in church, but that her spirit had floated away weightlessly into some peaceful silent land. There was no turmoil in that place, no endless anxiety, just an overwhelming sense of overall calm.

As Mandy's mind and her emotions began to adjust to this unearthly serenity, the stillness of that state was superseded by the sound of a strong voice. It was not a hard, or strident, or demanding voice. No, it was rather the confident voice of someone who had no doubts about his ability, no qualms about his claims.

"Jonathan is going to be well," it said. "He is in My hands. All you have to do is trust Me. Just trust Me."

With that the voice faded, and Mandy found herself returned, with the same gentle tenderness that she would return Jonathan to his pram or cot if she could only be permitted to do such a thing, to reality.

But she had missed part of the service during that strange, spiritual, supernatural experience! The pastor was by then standing in the pulpit reading the Scriptures prior to the presentation of his message. Mandy never heard a word of the man's message, either, though! For she had just been given another message, which she believed to have been a direct revelation from the Lord.

Jonathan was going to be well. All she had to do was trust Him!

Immediately the service was over Mandy nudged her husband who had begun his usual Sunday routine of nodding across to this one and waving across to that one, "Come on Jackie," she half-whispered half-shouted into his ear. "We have to get up to the hospital straight away!"

"Well, I mean… what do you mean?" Jackie began, bewildered. "What about Jack and Mina and the dinner, I mean…?"

"Oh Jackie, forget about Jack and Mina and your dinner, for once!" Mandy urged him. "The Lord has told me that Jonathan is going to be well!"

When he realized that Mandy meant what she said, Jackie eventually agreed to forego his dinner in the meantime, and drive her up to the Ulster Hospital.

As they made steady progress out of the city towards the hospital in the suburbs, and Jackie listened to Mandy going on and on about her 'out-of-the-body experience', and 'a sort of a trance', and 'the deep strong voice of the Lord' he was outwardly sympathetic, but inwardly sceptical.

"Yes, Mandy, that will be wonderful if it's true," he said.

'This is it. The pressure had got to her. I knew it had to, sometime. Mandy has flipped her lid at last!' he thought.

The moment of truth came when they entered the ward.

They were just dressing themselves up in the compulsory gowns, gloves and hats, when they noticed a nurse, whom they knew to be a Christian coming along towards them. When she saw Jackie and Mandy she almost broke into a run, and her face broke into a big broad smile.

"Oh Mr. and Mrs. Dickey, I have just been waiting for you to come up!" she called from at least ten yards distant. "I have wonderful news! Come with me!" and with that she led the gowned up couple into the premature baby unit.

"Look!" she exclaimed, trying vainly to appear calmly professional, despite her undisguised excitement. "We have been able to take Jonathan off the ventilator. Look! He is breathing on his own! We think he is going to make it!"

The young parents both burst into tears, simultaneously.

Jonathan is going to be well, was the message to Mandy in church.

And he was.

Three weeks later Mandy was allowed to realize one of her lifelong ambitions.

She experienced one of the supreme thrills of motherhood.

She held her now out of danger baby to her breast.

Again she wept, in wonder, in thanksgiving, and in virtual disbelief.

'Just trust Me,' the Voice had said.

'Just trust Me.'

Chapter Twenty-Four

CLOCKS

When baby Jonathan was well enough to be discharged from hospital, into the tender care of his proud mum and dad, Jackie realized that he would need to find himself a job, if possible, in order to help support his wife and infant son. He and Mandy had been advised that because of his very premature birth, Jonathan would be a child with special needs, and they both appreciated that the meeting of those special needs would almost inevitably mean at least some degree of added expense.

Since he was unable to afford the constant expense of the bus fare from Newtownards to Belfast in search of work, Jackie and Mandy applied to the Housing Executive for a house back in their native east Belfast.

Although the house in Newtownards made them a comfortable home, Jackie knew that his chances of obtaining employment would be better back home in the city, than in the County Down town. By that time there was no work to be had in the shipyard, which was actually decreasing rather than increasing its work force, but there were jobs available elsewhere.

After a short wait Jackie and Mandy were allocated a house in Solway Street, off the Newtownards Road. This they thought was a real answer to prayer, in the city, near their church, wonderful.

The young couple were thrilled to be granted the tenancy of such a house. It was a cosy, welcoming little street house, heated by an enclosed fire burning smokeless fuel.

We will be ever so happy here, they thought.

They were soon to discover, however, that daylight was the better part of any day in that house.

In the evening, when the house was warm, and the lights all went out at bedtime leaving the house clothed in comfortable cover, the companies of cockroaches all came out to conduct their nightly route march, all over the house.

It was not that there were only one or two of these horrible black bugs, 'clocks' as the locals called them. There were hundreds, maybe even thousands of them. Within weeks Jackie told Mandy that he believed that one quarter of all the 'clocks' in the city of Belfast, and at least three quarters of the total quota for the Newtownards Road, had come to live with them.

The house was infested.

And Jackie and Mandy were so worried for the health of their new, and at that time still delicate baby.

This plague of cockroaches became so bad that Jackie and Mandy hated going downstairs to the toilet during the hours of darkness. Every time you set your foot down it crunched the shell of a big black bug, and its feelers tickled the sole of your foot and sent a shiver snaking up your spine. It you decided to avoid this experience and keep a pair of slippers at the ready beside the bed they had to be left upside down, otherwise they would be full of more than your feet when you chose to use them.

It reminded Jackie of his jungle-training course with the Navy!

When he and Mandy contacted the Housing Executive office with their concerns about the ever-present cockroaches they promised to fumigate the house, which they did.

This abolished the cockroaches but left the house covered in a white choking dust.

And when, at the end of a week, the pungent smell of the insecticide had abated sufficiently to allow Jackie and Mandy to feel happy eating in the house again, the cockroaches returned, hordes of them, the same as ever.

So they prayed to God for help and guidance, and then contacted the Housing Executive again. And they fumigated the house again.

And in a week's time the 'clocks' were back, hordes of them, the same as ever.

In desperation Jackie and Mandy contacted their doctor. When he heard of their dilemma, and the conditions in which they were living, he wrote a letter to the Housing Executive, explaining that Jonathan had been a premature baby who was not long home from hospital, and needed to be raised in 'a healthy environment'

When Jackie presented this letter in the Housing Executive office in Ann Street, the lady with the ever so serious face assured him that they 'would attend to the situation as soon as possible'.

They did, too. They sent a man out the next day to fumigate the house again!

And at the end of another choking week making footprints in insecticide rather than taking footsteps on cockroaches, the hard-backed shiny-black invaders were back to resume their nightly forays all over the house.

Jackie and Mandy didn't know what to do.

They had asked for help, and the Housing Executive had, they said, done all they could.

They had prayed for guidance and still there had been no improvement in their situation. Was God testing their dependence upon Him, their patience with the housing authorities, or what?

After another three weeks of cockroach-crunching Jackie had decided he could take no more of it, and he told Jackie what he planned to do.

Mandy's immediate reaction was one of caution, stemming from their Christian commitment.

"Oh no, Jackie! You couldn't do that! We are Christians. What would they think about us?" she remonstrated.

"Could I not?" was Jackie's emphatic retort. "You'll see if I can't! And as for the bit about us being Christians, I have come to the conclusion, rightly or wrongly, that God sometimes helps only those who help themselves. And another wee thing! I don't know who 'they' are that you are talking about, so I don't care what 'they' think!"

He was well wound up, and ready to go!

Jackie was sufficiently psyched up to swing phase one of his plan into action.

Shortly before daybreak next morning, before the enemy had retreated to their daytime bunkers, Sailor Dickey set out on patrol again. This time he was not armed with an SLR, but with nothing more deadly than a small torch which had cost one-ninety nine in Woolworth's, a two-pound jampot with a screw-on lid, and the little shiny shovel from the companion-set on the hearth. His was not a shoot to kill policy, either, for the brief for his operation that night was to capture the enemy alive. They would be no good to him dead.

Later on that same morning, when all the workers had gone to work, Jackie Dickey took the bus into the city centre. He was clutching a common enough, innocent enough looking, plastic carrier bag. The other passengers in the bus, women with infants, and pensioners with problems, paid no notice to this very ordinary guy with his crumpled, obviously often carried, plastic bag.

When he reached his city centre stop, Jackie walked around to The Housing Executive office and demanded to see someone in authority. Eventually a senior lady came to speak to him.

"It's about this house we are living in," Jackie began, as he normally would have done. "I was wondering when you are going to do something about it or give us another house?"

The official-looking lady donned her official-looking glasses and peered into an official-looking file.

"Yes," she murmured at length, "I see you have a problem with cockroaches, Mr. Dickey. I also see by the notes here that we have fumigated the house twice. Or was it three times?"

"Yes we have a problem with cockroaches, you are right," Jackie agreed with her, warming to the subject. "And it was three times, but it hasn't done one bit of good."

The lady took off her glasses, set them upside down o the desk, and looked across at the troubled tenant before her. "I'm sorry, Mr. Dickey," she tried to tell him "we have done everything we can at present. There is nothing more we can do for you meantime."

Jackie Dickey was uncharacteristically calm. He didn't shout, or stamp, or fly into a rage. He merely reached into his battered bag, took out a two-pound jampot, and poured its contents, more than fifty shiny black adult cockroaches, on to the desk in front of her.

"Well in the meantime, as you say, when you are thinking about it, maybe you would like to live with those. We do, with our baby, every day, and every night."

The 'clocks' caused chaos in that office.

When they reached the end or the desk they just dropped off lemming-like, hit the floor with a clonk and set off scuttling in every direction. Within seconds the office staff, and the not cockroach accustomed customers were scuttling in every direction, too.

Jackie left his jampot on the desk, told them all to 'have a nice day', and walked out.

When he reached home, he recounted the details of his escapade to Mandy, who had never been one hundred per cent convinced about the ethics of the exercise. He ended his tale with a short laugh and a profound prediction. "We will get another house in a week or two, you'll see!" he prophesied.

And he was right! In just a little more than two weeks Jackie and Mandy received a letter to say that they had been allocated a house in Oval Street, near Glentoran's football ground, which was known as The Oval.

What a change this new house proved to be! It was warm, comfortable and clean. The lady who had been the previous tenant, and was reluctant to 'leave my wee house', as she described it, sold the incoming young couple all the carpets and curtains for the princely sum of twenty pounds!

On their first night in that house Jackie and Mandy thought that heaven couldn't really be much nicer than this. They could sleep so peacefully, without any cares about cockroaches.

For they soon found that there were only two clocks in that house in Oval Street. One was on the mantelpiece in the living room, and the other on the dressing table in the bedroom!

Chapter Twenty-Five

A WONDERFUL DAY!

During those dark autumn and early winter days of 1987, with Jonathan continuing to make steady physical progress, Jackie and Mandy were continuing to make steady progress also, in the spiritual realm.

Despite all the minor hiccups of cockroaches, housing, and the spectre of continued unemployment, Jackie and Mandy were so thankful to God for His goodness to them. As a token of their love and appreciation they were very keen to do something in the service of the Lord, something to help bring others to the Saviour. They wanted somehow to attempt to reach the people living around their streets with the good news of the Gospel.

Having considered a number of options, they decided, in January 1988, that their best plan, the way in which they could most effectively reach the most significant number of potentially receptive people, was to become involved in the organization of the youth work in their local church.

The young and enthusiastic couple enjoyed the work. Every Friday they wrapped Jonathan up warmly and took him down with them to the church hall where they had games and activities arranged for the young people, and a tuck shop where they could buy snacks. Each evening ended with the presentation of a simple Bible message, outlining the way of salvation to the young people, many of whom had never heard it before.

After Easter that year Jackie announced that he and Mandy would like to take all the young people who were regular attenders at the youth club for a day trip to the seaside town of Newcastle, County Down, on a Saturday in June.

"The only problem is," he said in the course of his explanation, "we know your parents probably couldn't afford a fiver to give you to pay for this day out, and we don't want to be asking the church for the money to pay for it. We think it would be a good idea if we could raise the money ourselves."

This proposal was immediately met by a chorus of suggestions, ranging from the possibly acceptable to the definitely unacceptable.

"Great idea, Jackie," everyone agreed. "We could look after people's babies… collect in the Con Club…do old women's messages…have a sponsored walk to Newtownards…"

Jackie held up his hand to stem the rising tide of recommendations.

"We are not making any decision tonight," he said, when the clamour had subsided sufficiently to allow him to say anything. "Go away and think about it, and next week we will settle on something."

And when next week came around Jackie and Mandy were confronted with a crowd of eager kids, all with more sensible ideas, for many of them had talked to parents and friends about possible fund-raising schemes.

After a session when everyone set out their ideas it was generally agreed that the most practical suggestion put forward was to have a car wash, on a Saturday, in the church car park. That could involve everybody and help the local motorists while all the time helping them to realize their aim, which was to raise money for an outing.

When the date and times for the youth club car wash were settled, for the last Saturday in May, from two o'clock until five o'clock in the afternoon, the organizing committee, which included everybody, was confronted by another problem.

How were they to advertise this special hands-on car wash?

"We will make posters and bring them next week," a number of the older and more innovative members volunteered. "Then you can go round the shops and places on the Road, Jackie, and put them in."

It was a good idea, and the keen young people proved to be very successful at designing posters. After they had brought them the next week, as promised, however, Jackie and his assistant, 'Big Jim' a lad of fourteen who was easily as tall as Jackie, had very little success in placing them in the local shops.

They were constantly rebuffed.

"We have no space for another poster", some said. "Just take a look at the windy in that door there already."

"We only place professional posters in our advertising space," some of the snooty ones said.

"We don't put up posters about church things," others said.

What a load of excuses!

When Jackie and Big Jim went back to the group next week they felt like failures.

Some of the younger members of the group had the answer to that problem too,

"Give the posters to us, Jackie. We will get them into all sorts of places, no problem," they assured the disgruntled leaders.

And they did!

Jackie was amazed when he visited a number of the local shops during the week and saw posters displayed in locations where he couldn't manage to place them.

"How on earth did you do it?" he couldn't wait to enquire the next Friday.

"Easily," one twelve-year-old girl told him. "All we had to do was go into the shops and things and tell the bosses that if they didn't put up our posters we would tell our mothers never to shop there again. Never ever. And it worked."

Then a boy of ten piped up. "There is even one in the 3-2-1 Bingo Hall, Jackie, for I went in there and told a fella that if he didn't put up my poster I would tell me ma and her friend Sadie never to go there again. They would be going with my Aunt Sally to her club on up the Road a bit!"

When the big day came, the afternoon of the last Saturday in May proved to be bright and sunny. There were lots of people about, and lots of people called at the car wash in the church car park and paid two pounds to have their vehicles washed by swarms of soaking kids who depended more on continual splashing and copious supplies of soapsuds for success than anything resembling an organized system.

They were not short of enterprise either. For on the few occasions when business flagged and there were no more cars left for them to wash, they lined themselves across the pedestrian crossing and blocked the busy main road until a few more motorists were persuaded that their particular cars could really do with a washing!

And when it came to half past five and the last car had driven out of the park, they were left with saturated clothes, squelching wellies, tired arms, and sunburnt happy faces.

They had, Jackie was in a position to inform them, raised more than enough money for a day out to Newcastle!

When the long anticipated day of the outing came around it turned out to be every bit as sunny, but just that little bit warmer, than the car-washing fund-raising day had been.

There was much excited chatter on the bus. All the young people were so thrilled at being away for the day, and the leaders were quite astonished to learn that some of these children had never been to the seaside before. Jackie sat with his second in command, Big Jim, and Mandy nursed Jonathan all the way, with Suzanne beside her. This girl was very special to Jackie and Mandy for she had been saved in the Youth Club, and was always eager to help. Though still only twelve years of age, Suzanne was intelligent, sensible and incredibly street-wise. She proved invaluable in helping communicate with the others, for she lived where they lived, understood their thinking, and spoke their language.

When the doors of the minibus opened in the Donard Park in Newcastle, shortly after one o'clock, Jackie gave every boy and girl some money to spend out of what they had earned three weeks before, and then told them to be back at four o'clock for tea.

Some of the children could barely wait for the instructions and if they hadn't been compelled to wait for their pocket money they would have been away long since. So Jackie hadn't finished saying, "Right now, off you go," until half of them were away with a whoop, across the street, along the promenade, and down on to the beach.

Jackie and Mandy had just finished locking up the minibus, and settling Jonathan in his buggy, when Big Jim came panting back. Between gasping for breath and laughing uncontrollably he could hardly speak.

"Come quick and see this!" he said, when he eventually recovered his composure enough to say something sensible. "The twins ran straight down the sand, and straight into the sea, clothes and all! And now they are splashing about in it having a whale of a time!"

Jackie and Mandy made their way down to the beach, and discovered that what Big Jim had said was true.

John and Stewart, the twins, and at nine years old, the youngest pair in the party, were frolicking about in the sea, fully clothed.

When he had reached the edge of the tide Jackie called them and they came paddling and plunging out.

"You are supposed to take your clothes off before you go into the sea, boys!" he called at them when they came within earshot.

"Oh are you?" Stewart said. "Nobody told us you were supposed to take your clothes off! But don't worry Jackie, we will take them off now!"

and with that he began to pull down his sea-soaked shorts.

"No! No! No! Just keep them on until we find you something else to wear!" he told them. Jackie knew that these lads had no inhibitions and would have been quite happy to take all their clothes off, and spend the remainder of the afternoon starkers on the shore.

Mandy then found that her first job of the outing was to leave Jonathan with Suzanne and search Newcastle street for two pairs of cheap swimming trunks, two T-shirts, and two pairs of shorts!

When she had returned, Mandy released Suzanne to 'go up the street to the shops,' if she wished, and then joined her husband in supervising the children who just did not want to leave the beach.

They ran on the warm sand.

They felt it below their feet.

They ran it through their fingers.

They paddled in the gentle, lightly-lapping waves.

They picked up shells and washed them in rock pools.

They threw slimy slivers of seaweed at each other.

It was a wonderful revelation, and a marvellous reward to Jackie and Mandy, to see these children, from the streets of the city, revelling in every new surprise of the seashore.

When it came four o'clock and time for tea, everyone was treated to chips and a can of Coke, not exotic fare, but what the children all said they wanted.

As they sat on the wall in the sunshine, eating their tea Mandy was again beside Suzanne, and noticing that her willing aide had acquired a blue plastic bag bearing a gift shop label, she asked, "Did you buy yourself something nice, Suzanne?"

"No, I didn't," came the frankly honest reply. "I just bought a wee ornament for my mammy."

"That was very kind of you," Mandy went on, "but are you not going to buy yourself something, too?"

Suzanne hung her head, and blushed red below her sunburn. "I can't," she replied, with her unashamed honesty. "I have spent all my money on that."

And she lifted her blue bag six inches.

Mandy was touched.

Here was a girl who had worked as hard, if not harder, than all the others to make this outing possible, and she had spent every penny of the pocket money she had been given, on a present for her mother!

There was money left, Mandy knew, so she opened her purse and slipped Suzanne a five-pound note. "That last money you were given was your pocket money," she stumbled to explain. "This I am giving you now is your pay, for helping Jackie and me. Go now and spend at least some of it on yourself."

Suzanne blushed again, and refused to take the money, but eventually, when pressed, she did. And bought something for herself.

Seven o'clock was to have been time to leave for home, but nobody, not even the leaders, wanted to leave the sun-drenched seaside resort so early on such a beautiful evening. So it was almost eight-thirty before everyone was rounded up, and checked and rechecked on to the minibus and then they were ready to leave Newcastle for the Newtownards Road.

As they travelled home Mandy noticed that many of the children were holding bags of different sizes in sweaty, sandy, chip-smelly hands.

"Did you buy yourself something?" she asked one boy.

"No. It's not for me. It's for my mammy," was his reply.

"I see you have been shopping," she remarked to another, a girl.

"Aye. It's just a wee thing for my mammy," she replied.

Even John and Stewart, the twins, each had a long narrow brown-paper bag poking out of the top of the plastic bag containing his salted clothes. The smaller bag contained 'just a stick of rock for my mammy.'

It almost seemed that Jackie or Mandy or somebody in authority had told these young people to buy something 'for their mammy'! But they hadn't. It was just something that the children had wanted to do instinctively.

As they spilled out of the minibus, in the more familiar surroundings of the church car park, with the sun setting behind the shipyard cranes, every single one of those young people came across to Jackie and Mandy, and said, in his or her own particular way, " Thank you very much! That was a wonderful day!"

When they were free to drive round home Jackie and Mandy flopped down into chairs, tired but thrilled.

It had been a wonderful day for them, too, but perhaps for a slightly different reason.

And that was that they had learnt some more wonderful things about some wonderful kids.

Chapter Twenty-Six

UNRECOGNISABLE

In the spring of 1989 Jackie and Mandy sold their bungalow in Newtownards and moved from Oval Street to a house which they had bought in Dunraven Park, off Grand Parade, in their native east Belfast.

God poured out further blessings on the lives of the young couple who were so keen to please Him, and be profitable for Him, in a couple of other ways that year also.

Jackie at last found permanent employment in a Co-op general store close to his home during the summer, and in September Jackie and Mandy's first daughter, Danielle was born. Jonathan, who was by then more than two years old, had progressed far beyond medical expectations. And now he had a baby sister!

During those days, Jackie, who had felt he must leave the Ulster Defence Regiment, because of his addiction to alcohol, but had seen his life completely transformed by the power of God, felt led by that same God to work amongst military personnel. He wanted to contact them for Christ, showing them what compassion and care he could, in the name of Jesus, and sharing his faith with them. So he began by devoting most of his spare time to visiting soldiers in their barracks, and also in hospital.

One afternoon, in May 1993, Jackie was walking out of the military wing of Musgrave Park Hospital, having called to see a soldier friend who had broken a leg playing football, and he was greeting some of the other patients as he passed.

Suddenly he heard a voice call his name.

"Is that you, Sailor?" it enquired.

Jackie stopped and was retracing the few steps to look into the side ward which he had just passed when the call was repeated.

"Is that you, Sailor?" it enquired.

When he came to the door of the side ward, Jackie stopped again. There were four beds in there, but he didn't recognize any of the patients.

He was just about to turn and walk away again, convinced that his ears had been playing tricks on him, when the same voice spoke again. It came from the bed in the far left hand corner.

"Sailor, it's me. I'm over here. I saw you going past there and called you," it said.

When he had crossed the ward to the bed in the corner, Jackie saw that this particular patient had stitches all over his face. Congealed blood lay caked in irregular reddish black lines where the stitched wounds had been drawn together.

Jackie's instant reaction was one of revulsion. This man's face was like something out of a horror film.

And still Jackie didn't recognize the man in the bed.

And the man in the bed realized immediately that his erstwhile friend hadn't recognized him.

"It's Sammy," he informed Jackie, his voice breaking.

Sammy had remained in the U.D.R., whose name had by then been changed to the Royal Irish Regiment.

"And what happened you, Sammy?" his former patrol partner, and holiday companion, went on to ask, tenderly. Jackie was shocked to see the state of Sammy's face, and being lost for words, made the natural enquiry out of something to say.

"They got me at last, Sailor," the patient went on to explain. "I was shot in the face in the Markets area the day before yesterday."

"Oh I'm so sorry, Sammy," Jackie was instantly sympathetic. He knew that the very same thing could have happened to him some years before.

Then he switched from sympathy to apology.

"I'm awful sorry I didn't know you there, Sammy," he stumbled to cover his confusion. "But with all the blood around your face I just didn't know who it was that had called me."

"I'm not surprised you didn't know me, Sailor. Even my wife here didn't know me the first time she came up to see me," and with that Sammy waved an arm across to indicate the woman sitting sadly at the other side of the bed.

Then there was a long, awkward silence.

Jackie didn't know what to say next, Sammy's wife just sat staring vacantly into space, and Sammy began to cry.

This had a singular, and sinister, sequel.

As the tears welled up in his eyes and overflowed onto his cheeks, they mingled with the hardened blood. And softened it.

Sammy's wife bent forward to wipe them away but had to desist. Her husband squealed out in pain.

And so, as Jackie stood there, feeling incredibly helpless, great sticky clots of congealed blood, like blobs of half-set raspberry jelly, flowed down Sammy's face and stained the starched white sheet, pulled up around him.

All at once, standing transfixed and tearful by the side of that bed, Jackie Dickey was whisked back in time. In a split second vision he saw a man on a cross. Blood was flowing, then slowing, in clots and blobs down His face from a crown of thorns which had been hammered fiercely into His forehead. With the mask of stiffening blood the victim's features were indistinguishable.

He was unrecognisable.

Jackie recalled a Bible verse he had heard a pastor quote in a meeting once. It was about that crucified man. As far as he could remember it said, 'His visage was so marred more than any man...'

The hospital visitor had come to try and bring comfort and cheer to others.

Now he was challenged himself. Bowing his head he used the side of a clenched fist to wipe the tears from his chin, and then said, under his breath,

"Thank you Lord, for dying for me.

Thank you Lord for Calvary's tree,

Thank you Lord, for bringing to me,

Your great salvation so rich, and free."

Then he opened his eyes, and spoke to the man in the mess in the bed. The Saviour who had saved Sailor could save Sammy, too. And Sailor had to tell him that.

"Although you are in a bit of a state, Sammy, God has been good to you, for He has spared your life. You could have died there in the street. Or in the ambulance. Or in the intensive care ward. But you didn't," he tried to console him. "God has spared you for your wife and wee girl. But maybe He is trying to tell you something, too, Sammy."

"Yes I know that, Sailor," Sammy admitted. "God hasn't allowed me to die. And maybe He is trying to tell me something. I would like to give my life to Him from now on. Will you pray for me?"

"Yes, I will, Sammy," and Jackie prayed simply for his friend, asking God to help him trust in Christ for salvation.

"When he had finished, Sammy squeezed his hand and said, "Thanks, Sailor. I have done that."

Jackie then wiped away yet another tear, and promised Sammy that he would be back.

And he did go back, twice or three times every week.

On one of his visits Jackie brought his friend who was improving physically, something to help satisfy his increasing spiritual appetite.

It was a special copy of the New Testament with Psalms, which he had arranged to have adorned with the crest of the Royal Irish Regiment.

Sammy was pleased with it, and read it avidly during the long days of his slow and painful recovery. And Jackie derived great pleasure from explaining to him some of the wonderful blessings that were his as a child of God, the son of a King.

As he left the hospital one evening about six weeks after the night of the first encounter, Jackie smiled to himself. It was a warm, pleasant, July evening, and it reminded him of their holiday in Majorca.

That morning when he had told his friends about his newly found faith in Christ it had been Sammy who had asked Jackie if he had 'lost his head'.

Sammy had also been the one who had prophesied that 'Sailor will never stick it' predicting that he would be 'back on the booze in about a month.'

But now the God who had saved Sailor, had saved Sammy, too.

And the God who had kept Sailor, could keep Sammy, too.

Chapter Twenty-Seven

'P' IS FOR PRAY

Although still working in the Co-Op every day, to help pay the bills, Jackie continued to spend more and more of his leisure time in hospital visitation, both amongst military personnel and others. From the time of his father's illness and hospitalisation he had realized that there were so may sick people craving for comfort, and often for company, and also seeking some source of solace. There were also so many wounded servicemen and women who were in need not only of physical restoration but also of a spiritual transformation. They urgently required both the healing of their bodies and the salvation of their souls.

With his frequent, and tactful, programme of visitation in the Ulster Hospital, Dundonald, the regular staff came to know Jackie, and they would occasionally tell him of particularly lonely, or otherwise needy patients who they thought would appreciate a visit.

One afternoon in January 1994 he was passing the Intensive Care Unit in that hospital when he met David who was the nurse in charge of the unit, and also a Christian.

"A young Military Policewoman was admitted here yesterday, Jackie," he informed the visitor. "If you like I will speak to the guards to allow you a minute or two to pray with her."

"O.K. David. I will do that," Jackie volunteered, not knowing what to expect.

The supervising nurse spoke to the two Military Policemen on duty at the ward door, explaining that Jackie was an ex-serviceman and well known in the hospital for his visitation. He was a 'kind of a chaplain' and he could be trusted. Since the young policewoman was from England and would have no affiliation with any local church, would it be in order, he wondered, if Jackie could 'say a short prayer with her'?

The policemen had no objections and Jackie was admitted to the ward.

And what a pathetic scene met his eyes!

Jayne, (not her real name), the young woman in the bed, had been shot four times, twice in the head, once in the chest, and once in the side. Her head was enclosed in a metal cage to keep it steady, and tubes and wires of various sizes, lengths and colours, entered and left the bed at strategic points.

A medical team of a nurse and two doctors was working with her, and two women, whom Jackie was later to discover were Jayne's mother and older sister, sat in a numbed trance on either side of the bed.

Jackie stood stock still, feeling something of an intruder upon an intense and intimate struggle for survival.

As he waited for the doctors to complete their immediate treatment, Jackie was beset by a horrible thought.

An Irishman has shot this lovely English girl, it said, and how can you, another Irishman have the downright cheek to stand by her bedside and tell her God loves her? It's preposterous. Incongruous. Ridiculous.

His instant reaction was to turn and walk out.

How could he have the face to...?

Then he realized that the argument implanted in his mind had been a subtle ploy of the devil to thwart him in his work. God had led him miraculously into that situation. And He would help him through it.

So he stayed where he was.

In a few minutes time the medical team had finished their work with Jayne and Jackie stepped forward. When he had introduced himself to her mother and sister, he spoke to the girl in the bed.

"My name in Jackie Dickey," he began. "I used to be in the Navy and the U.D.R. I am now in Civvy Street but as a Christian I visit in the hospitals and David asked me to come in to see you. I am going to give your sister a New Testament for you, and then I will pray with you, if that is O.K."

As Jackie produced one of his specially inscribed Testaments from his pocket he noticed that Jayne was lifting her right hand laboriously up off the covers. Her left arm, which was on the side with the bullet wound, lay limp and motionless.

He gave the New Testament across to the shocked sister, who said, "I think she wants to say something to you. Take the hand she is holding up. That is how she has been communicating with us since last night. By spelling words into our hands."

When he did as instructed, Jackie was amazed to find that Jayne did indeed want to send him a message. Using the index finger of her right hand she traced a capital 'P' on the palm of his hand. Then she did it again. And again.

For a minute Jackie was taken aback.

"She is making the letter 'P' on my hand," he said to the patient's anxious mother and sister. "What could that mean?"

It was mother who came up with the answer.

"'P' probably means pray," she suggested simply.

Jackie was touched and also rather chastened that he hadn't thought of it first.

"That's right," he agreed. "'P' is for pray."

Aware that Jayne was critically ill, and also that the doctors would soon be returning, Jackie wasted no more time.

Holding her hand, he began to pray for her, and as he prayed he was conscious of the warmth of the love of God for the wounded girl, pervading both his body and mind and helping him choose the right words to say.

When he had finished praying Jackie assured Jayne's mother and sister that he would be back to see her, and was preparing to leave, when the older sister said, "I will give her the little book."

She then reached across and placed the New Testament with its inscribed insignia in the semi-conscious Jayne's only useable hand.

A tear came into Jackie's eye when he saw what happened next. Slowly, and obviously painfully, she moved the New Testament across and pressed it tightly against the bullet wound in her chest.

As he turned to leave the bed, Jackie heard the lovely girl, who was battling for life, murmur, "Mummy, mummy, mummy," very softly.

And then she lapsed into unconsciousness.

Through the unquestionable skill and unstinting dedication of the medical staff, and no doubt as an answer to the many earnest prayers of Jackie and friends in the Church, Jayne survived.

In little more than a week she was moved from Intensive Care out on to a side ward, and then eventually on to Ward 19.

Jackie became a regular, and welcome visitor to her bedside, as she recovered.

On good days, when Jayne was not in too much pain, or afflicted by too many distressing mental images, Jackie read to her from her little New

Testament which she kept proudly displayed on her locker. He then took every opportunity to tell her of the love of God, of the death of Christ, of forgiveness for sins, and of the need to trust in Jesus.

It was patient, painstaking work, for Jayne had never heard the message of the Gospel, set out in all its simplicity, before.

Jackie found it particularly encouraging on the days when Jayne had a question to ask him about some remark he had made on a previous visit.

She had been thinking about the matter, obviously, and Jackie prayed privately all the more earnestly, that she would not only think about it but also do something about it.

There were other days, though, when Jayne was not in a position to talk about anything. On those days she just lay and sobbed. She had been having flashbacks to the day of her attempted murder, and seemed incapable of banishing those horrendous pictures from her mind.

On such occasions Jackie remained only briefly, holding her hand for solace, and praying for strength to enable her to overcome the frightening flashbacks.

After she had been in the Ulster Hospital for a number of weeks, Jayne told Jackie that she wouldn't be seeing him again for she was being moved back to England, to a specially equipped hospital in Leeds, for rehabilitation, the next day. She thanked Jackie for his attention, for his prayers, and for the little New Testament, which she promised to read.

Jackie told her that he was glad she was well enough to go home, and that he would continue to pray for her. He then took what he knew would probably be his last opportunity to speak to her about the Lord who meant so much to him.

"Remember what I have been telling you, Jayne," he said as they parted. "God loves you, Jesus died on the cross to put away your sins, and He is calling you to come and trust in Him. Just open your heart and let Him in to take control of your life, the way I told you I did years ago."

Although he now knows little of Jayne's physical condition or spiritual position, Jackie still keeps the promise he made to her.

He prays for her every day, often recalling that January afternoon in the Intensive Care Ward as he does so.

For that was where he was challenged by a simple lesson from the alphabet.

'P' is for pray', was what he learnt.

Chapter Twenty-Eight

KNOCK, KNOCK ... WHO'S THERE?

Jackie found it a big challenge to return to Palace Barracks, Holywood, as a changed man.

When last based there, he had been a serving soldier, dreading death when on duty, and usually drunk when off it. And it was there, too, that he had once attempted to take his own life, to end it all.

Now, though, when he visited the barracks, it was as a totally different character, and in a totally different capacity. Since his life had been turned around by the grace and power of God, Jackie was attempting to tell as many people as possible, including those men and women still working there, about the good news of the Gospel. And the transformation in his life had to be, for those who had known him before, a tangible proof of the positive nature of the message.

Having made a number of calls at the army base, he became aware of a wonderful opportunity to tell others of his Saviour. There were a number of children living in the base, sons and daughters of serving soldiers, and Jackie and Mandy applied for permission to start a Sunday School amongst them. This permission was granted and the pair became weekly visitors to the base, speaking to thirty or forty boys and girls every Sunday.

This regular association with Palace Barracks allowed Jackie to form a meaningful friendship with some of the soldiers who were stationed there.

During the summer of 1994, one of the men he met, and began talking to, was Private David Campbell.

Although a fully trained soldier, David had an interesting job in the camp. He was a groom. It was his responsibility to care for the twenty horses, which the regiment kept for use on different, and very often ceremonial, occasions.

On Sundays, when they had time after Sunday School, and it was suitable, Jackie and Mandy would take Jonathan and Danielle down to the stables to see the horses. And there they often saw David.

And on a weekday, when Jackie was in the barracks to visit the service men and women, many of whom were under a strain that he well understood, he always called down to the stables to see David. And there he often saw the horses.

Unlike his children, whose prime object was to stand and gaze at the powerful shiny, well-groomed animals, Jackie's main concern was to contact the affable groom, and tell him about the Lord Jesus, the only one who could give him lasting peace in a trying and turbulent world.

During the autumn and winter months Jackie spoke to David a number of times, sharing with him, in a simple way, the truth of the Gospel, but David, though always courteous, never seemed to made any visible response.

Jackie liked the pleasant lad, nonetheless, and kept praying for him, and speaking to him as the opportunity arose.

Then on Thursday 2nd February, 1995, Jackie was on a routine visit to the base, and found David with a huge yard brush in his hand. He had just finished cleaning out the stables and was on his final brush-up.

As he crossed the yard to speak to him, Jackie could see that the young man was trembling. His hands and arms were shaking, causing the bristles of the brush to make wavy lines in the dirt.

When Jackie arrived within earshot, David had a question for him. Dispensing with all introductory formalities about the weather, or the state of his or anyone else's health, he launched straight into his enquiry.

"Jackie, does the Lord only knock for so long?" was what he was anxious to know.

"Yes, David," Jackie replied, sensing a deep sincerity in the question he had just been asked. "He only knocks for so long."

Looking up from the ground to look the visitor straight in the face, David went on to explain his concern.

"You see, I believe the Lord has been speaking to me for weeks, Jackie. And I haven't been listening. My life has been upside-down for a long time, I have felt so mixed-up, so unsettled, and I wondered at first what was causing it. Then it dawned on me. Jesus is going knock, knock, knock, at the door of my life. And I haven't been opening," he told the attentive Jackie, who recognized at once that God was calling the heartbroken groom with the shaking handled broom.

When he had offered an instant and inward prayer for guidance in dealing with this stricken soul, Jackie spoke again, softly, earnestly.

"You know that I have been speaking to you about Jesus for nearly a year now, David," he began. "And it is Jesus who is knocking at the door of your life, as you say. But you must remember, that Jesus will not always knock. He might knock for a long time, but He may not knock forever. And He won't break the door down either. You will have to open it, and let Him in…"

"I know that, Jackie," was David's immediate and eager, almost urgent, response, breaking in on his friend's discourse. "But what I don't know, and what I want you to tell me is, why am I finding it so hard? I just don't seem to be able to drag that door open!"

That required some explanation, too. But Jackie had the answer.

"It is because the devil doesn't want to lose you," he told him. "He is trying to stop you trusting in Christ. He is making it a struggle for you. But you will have to make up your mind to trust in the Lord Jesus. Believe in Him and be saved. In other words, open the door."

When he glanced across at David, after this further gentle exhortation, Jackie noticed that the young man had begun to cry. Big tears had started to roll down his cheeks.

Knowing that he would not want to be seen weeping, Jackie said to him, "Come on over into the office David, and we can talk there."

When they had settled away from the bustle of the yard, and any possible disturbance, David said, "Jackie, I am not going to put it off any longer. I want the Lord to come into my life today."

Jackie produced a Bible from his pocket and read three verses from it to the disturbed young soldier.

The first was, 'All have sinned and come short of the glory of God.'

The next was one which he and Mandy had been teaching to the boys and girls in the Sunday School on the base. It was, 'For God so loved the world that he gave his only begotten Son, that whosoever believeth in him should not perish, but have everlasting life.'

And the final verse was the one which had immediately sprung into Jackie's mind when David had spoken about Jesus knocking at the door of his life. It was, 'Behold, I stand at the door and knock: if any man hear my voice, and open the door, I will come in to him, and will sup with him, and he with me.'

When he had closed the Bible gently, Jackie said, "Now I am going to pray, David, and when I have finished you can pray, asking Jesus to come into your heart."

And that was exactly what happened.

Jackie had just said his 'Amen', and was lifting his head to wink open an eye to see what David was doing when the groom began.

"Dear Lord, I am a sinner, and I need You for my Saviour. I know that You died for my sins and I am asking you now to come into my heart and into my life and to live with me always," was his simple, but profoundly sincere, prayer.

Jackie was overjoyed.

This was another answer to his prayers, for he had just seen another soul born into the kingdom of God.

Jesus had knocked.

David had opened.

Peace had entered.

Joy had arrived.

Chapter Twenty-Nine

SOLD

In early 1998 Jackie and Mandy were facing another, more practical, problem in their lives. Their present home had become too small for their growing family, for by then their third child, Hannah, had been born, and a fourth was expected.

They needed something more spacious. And they needed it soon.

Having three children meant that either parent had to spend some time occasionally with one or other of the children, staying away with relatives.

It was not ideal.

And when a new baby arrived it would be totally unsatisfactory.

Jackie and Mandy knew that. But they knew one or two other things as well.

They knew that they weren't rich, so they couldn't afford a flashy place.

They knew, and had proved, also, however, that they had a bountiful God who could, since He was the creator and controller of all things, provide them with somewhere suitable.

So they prayed about it. Earnestly.

There was just one limiting condition to their choice. In addition to the basic requirement of being large enough to hold a family of six, it 'would be good' if it could be close to Orangefield Primary School where the two older children had already been enrolled.

One May day, as they were driving along one of the arterial roads in east Belfast, they passed a house with an estate agent's 'For Sale' notice on it. It was the type of house they had always fancied, and just the right size to accommodate an expanding family.

The only problem was that suspended on two tiny chains from the main 'For Sale' sign, was another telltale little board.

It said, 'SOLD'.

Jackie and Mandy went home and talked to each other about it.

Always aware that it was not within their power to do anything about the matter, since they had no influence in the world of men, they proceeded to talk to their Lord about it. For they were convinced that He had.

In a simple, honest way, they presented the need to Him.

"Lord," they said, "that's just the sort of a house that we want, in just the sort of place we want. It is near to the children's Primary School, and we are sure that it would be big enough for all of us."

Then they made a further impassioned plea.

"If that is not the house for us, Lord," they asked, "please could You guide us to one somewhere in that area."

In July, their fourth child, and third daughter, Rebekah was born. Now they were a happy family of mum, dad, and four children, one of whom was a newborn baby, and their present accommodation was by far too small for all of them.

Then the miracle happened.

The need for a new home had progressed from being desirable to being desperate. From being merely beneficial to being absolutely vital.

Driving down that same road, one afternoon in early August they were surprised, and pleased, to see that the 'For Sale' sign had been reinstated in the garden of the house which they felt they had 'missed' before. The difference this time was, though, that the little soul-sickening 'SOLD' sign had vanished! It wasn't there any more!

The house was 'on the market' again.

Jackie and Mandy contacted the estate agent's office without delay.

"Yes," someone assured the eager couple. "That house is for sale again. The previous purchasers have pulled out."

With an excited expectation they made arrangements 'to call and view the property'. It all sounded so formal.

When they had been to see the house, with its owners the next day, the couple with the four kids decided that this was the house for them. This was the house to which God had guided them, they believed.

Only one obstacle remained, but unfortunately it was a big one.

It was called the price.

Having done their sums, and talked to various mortgage and insurance agents, and their Bank manager, Jackie and Mandy arrived at an amount, an absolute maximum figure, which they felt they could afford for what they considered to be their dream and God sent home. It had everything they wanted, and where they wanted it.

But the figures didn't match.

No matter how they tried, Jackie or Mandy or any one of a million managers couldn't have made their money add up to the minimum price that the buyers claimed they 'would need'.

They were at least three thousand pounds short.

There followed a short but stressful standoff.

Jackie and Mandy were so sure that it was God's will that they were to live in that particular house that they asked the church members to pray for God's guidance and intervention.

And within a week the would-be sellers of the house were on the telephone to the prospective buyers to tell them that they could purchase the property for the figure they could afford. They needed a quick sale for their new house across town was almost ready for occupation. Could Jackie and Mandy arrange for the deposit to be paid soon?

The deposit! Where were they going to find the deposit until all the arrangements for the disposal of their present property could be finalised?

When they went to discuss the matter with their Bank manager he pointed out to them that Jackie had a maturing insurance policy which had come due for payment the previous month.

As it so happened the lump sum, including a terminal bonus, proved just sufficient to provide the deposit!

So before the end of August, the SOLD sign returned to swing again below the For Sale notice on the tilted pole at the gate.

The new owners were Jackie and Mandy who were astonished at the speed with which the entire transaction had taken place.

And in mid-September they moved into their more spacious new home, within walking distance of Orangefield Primary School, with Jonathan, Danielle, Hannah, and baby Rebekah.

God had led, guided, and provided. Again.

How they praised Him!

Chapter Thirty

THE HERO GOES HOME

Settling into their new house was exciting for everyone except Rebecca, who didn't know much about it. Her main interests were still feeding when she was hungry and sleeping when she wasn't, and where she did those things didn't really matter.

For the others, though, there was so much to be done, so many matters to be seen to. Living rooms had to be organised and furnished, and bedrooms allocated and then decorated in keeping with the needs of a maturing boy with more than just normal needs, two growing girls, and a baby. Each of the older three had very definite ideas about which room should be his or her own special room with space for his or her own special stuff.

It was an interesting, absorbing time.

Jackie and Mandy were happy to be busy, catering for the family with which God had blessed them, in the home with which He had blessed them.

Then, in November, Jackie heard some distressing news.

He knew that brother Alex, his homecoming hero and boyhood idol, had been ill for some time, but didn't really realize the serious nature of his complaint.

It was his mother who told him that 'Alex has to go in for 'a big operation' on his throat in December.' It sounded ominous.

The entire family was concerned for Alex, but brother Jackie was concerned in an especially caring way, for his concern extended beyond filial compassion, to spiritual need. He was well aware that his brother was not a Christian, and his prospects of a return to a healthy life were not good.

Jackie prayed constantly and fervently that God would not only guide the surgeons in the operation, and that Alex would recover, but also that his older brother would be led to trust in Christ as his Saviour.

During the early months of 1999, just after the operation, Alex seemed to be making satisfactory progress, and then the problem, and the pain, returned. It came as a cruel shock to the family to be told in May that everything which could possibly have been done for Alex, medically, had been done.

No further treatment was possible.

That was it. End of story.

Jackie was devastated.

It distressed him to think of his brother so ill, with no spiritual solace in the present, and no possible prospect for the future.

In June the very ill man was admitted to the Marie Curie Cancer Care Centre, not far from Jackie's home.

This proximity allowed Alex's brother to place his name right at the top of his priority list of patients to call upon. He visited his big brother at least three times every week, and each and every visit disturbed him more than the one before.

Alex was sinking slowly.

Late one evening Jackie had a telephone call from his niece, Gillian. She knew that he would appreciate the purpose of her call for he had, on more than one occasion, shared with her his deep and genuine concern for his ailing brother.

"Uncle Jackie, I was wondering if it would be all right to ask my minister, Rev. David Mc Ilveen, to call with Uncle Alex when he is up visiting in the Marie Curie Centre? He is up there quite regularly, apparently," was what she wanted to know.

"That would be great, Gillian," Jackie was happy to reply. "I have tried dozens of times to get speaking to Alex on his own about spiritual things, but have never been able to manage it. He either seems to be in pain and sedated, or else there is somebody else there. Your minister might get a chance to speak to him on his own sometime."

The prospect of another caring Christian minister calling in on his brother pleased Jackie more than he could express, and Gillian promised to arrange it.

Alex seemed to like Rev. Mc Ilveen when he called. There was something about his deep sincerity and genuine care that appealed to the very ill patient, for whom speaking had by then become a very trying and painful process.

And in less than a month Gillian was back on the phone with wonderful news. Rev. Mc Ilveen had just called her to let her know that he had been up to see her Uncle Alex and been privileged to point him to Christ as Saviour.

What an answer to prayer! Jackie just stood and wept, the receiver still pressed close to his ear.

"That's great, Gillian. That's great!" he kept repeating when he had recovered sufficient composure to say anything.

It was indeed great, but as he considered that marvellous answer to the ardent prayers of many for Alex, Jackie realized that there was just one more thing he would like to happen.

Perhaps, he thought, it might even be a wee bit selfish, but I would really love to hear the momentous news from Alex himself.

So he prayed even more fervently, "Lord please grant me some time, even a short time, alone with Alex, when I can speak to him about You."

And God answered that prayer also.

Early in the evening of Wednesday 11 th August Jackie went up to call with Alex, bringing him some ice cream which he always loved. It was so soothing, and so easily swallowed.

When Jackie had begun to feed his brother slowly with the ice-cream, small spoonful after small spoonful, his sister Marie who was there with her husband Harry said, "We will go home for a while Jackie, now that you are here. We will be back later on."

And with that they left.

At last! Jackie and Alex had been left alone, and Alex was awake, and alert.

When he had finished feeding his brother with the much-appreciated ice cream, Jackie left the empty carton down on the bedside locker, and picked up the Gideon Bible which was lying there.

"I'm going to read a bit to you, Alex, if that's O.K." he said.

It was O.K. with Alex, for he nodded his head, as far as his failing strength and the depth of the pillow would permit.

Jackie had been waiting for this opportunity. He had gone over it in his mind dozens of times, so he knew what he wanted to read.

The first Bible passage he turned to was Psalm twenty-three.

And he read that down reverently, conscious that Alex was listening to every word.

Then he flicked over to John chapter fourteen. And read,

'Let not your heart be troubled: you believe in God, believe also in me. In my Father's house are many mansions... I go to prepare a place for you...'

What a comfort if you were a Christian!

'Jesus said unto him, I am the way, the truth and the life: no man comes unto the Father, but by me.'

What a challenge if you weren't!

Before he closed the Bible there was one more verse which Jackie felt he should read. It was in Romans chapter ten. This was his final verse for his brother,

'And whosoever shall call upon the name of the Lord shall be saved.'

Holding the Bible which he had just closed in one sweaty hand, he held his brother Alex's cold and skinny hand with the other one, and without further ado, began to pray.

It was one of those soft, tearful prayers, where the few words said were every one laden with sincerity and sentiment. Then when he had opened and wiped his watering eyes, Jackie looked straight at his brother, and put to him the question he had been longing to ask for weeks.

"Tell me this, Alex, do you know Jesus as your Saviour?" he enquired, tenderly.

There was a short silence.

Alex had closed his eyes again, and was lying completely still, just as he had been doing during his brother's prayer.

Then a faint smile, like a flash of heaven, crossed his lips. He nodded his head as far as his faint strength and the depth of the pillow would permit, for a second time.

And then he used all the power he could muster in the thin hand which Jackie was holding, and reversing the grip, he squeezed Jackie's as tightly as he could.

And that was enough.

That simple, silent gesture was all that was required.

For with that squeeze of the hand from his dying brother, Jackie knew that all was well with him. Whatever happened to either of them, they would meet again in heaven.

For the next four days Alex's condition continued to deteriorate and the family took it in turns to sit with him, day and night.

Strangely, though, when it came Jackie's turn for the bedside vigil, he didn't seem to mind it as much as he thought he would have done.

Death, for Alex, would now come as a welcome relief from constant pain, and a welcome release into a pain free, immortal kingdom.

And that release came just after daybreak on the following Sunday morning.

The slanting rays of the late summer sun had just begun to bathe the ward in a warm orange light when Alex Dickey passed away, surrounded by many softly weeping members of his family.

The homecoming hero had left to go home to be with his Lord.

And that could only be better.

OTHER BOOKS BY THE SAME AUTHOR

MY FATHER'S HAND

THIS IS FOR REAL

JUST THE WAY I AM

SOME PARTY IN HEAVEN

FIRST CITIZEN SMYTH

SOMETHING WORTH LIVING FOR

HOW SWEET THE SOUND

AS OUR HEADS ARE BOWED

ONLY THE BEST WILL DO

A BRUISED REED

BACK FROM THE BRINK

OUT OF THE MAZE

THE TANGLED LAMB